Advance Praise for Brian Tracy's *Full Engagement!*

"Brian Tracy's *Full Engagement!* is an extraordinary book, loaded with practical tools and ideas that every manager needs to be more effective and make the team feel terrific about themselves."

> —Mark C. Thompson, bestselling author of *Now Build a Great Business!* and *Success Built to Last*

"*Full Engagement!* is a fantastic journey that gives the reader great insights into how a manager's behaviors will affect the intrinsic motivation of staff, and, ultimately, the bottom line."

> —Joseph Sherren, President, Ethos Enterprises Inc.; CEO, Gateway Leadership Inc.; author, *iLead, Five Insights for Building Sustainable Organizations*; coauthor, *Vitamin "C" for a Healthy Workplace*

"Brian Tracy is one of the most practical and helpful advisers that I have ever met. *Full Engagement!* contains ideas that we can immediately apply—at work and at home."

> —Marshall Goldsmith, author of the *New York Times* bestsellers *MOJO* and *What Got You Here Won't Get You There*

"Leave it up to Brian Tracy to author another brilliant and to-the-point book on investing in people, fueling talent, and inspiring greatness! The magical way in which Brian explains and describes the importance of being happy and fueling happiness is right on target. In this time of recession and some diminished spirit in folks, he inspires and guides us to reflect on our own inner value and reminds us we can recession-proof ourselves by our actions, habits, and commitments. I highly recommend this book for anyone who manages and leads people, or if you are just looking for a great read to motivate and lead yourself!"

> —Steve Rodgers, President/Owner, Windermere Exclusive Properties, San Diego

"Brian Tracy has done it again! He has brought his insightful and intuitive wisdom to *Full Engagement!*, providing the tools necessary to positively influence and impact the people you lead. Read it, apply it, and rejoice in the results!"

> —Michael Clayton, President and CEO, The Better Business Bureau in Southeast Texas

"On a scale from 1 to 10, from very unhappy to very happy, I am 10+ with *Full Engagement!*. Yet another true work of art by Mr. Tracy, this book provides me with a whole host of proven best practices to bring the best out of my people and me. I cannot wait to incorporate these techniques with my department and help make the best people get better while they achieve greatness. Thanks Brian!"

—Matt Fenn, Senior Manager, Jostens Memory Book Training and Development

"Brian shows managers how to make people feel terrific about themselves and perform at their best."

—Keith Scott, founder, Beachcomber Hot Tubs

"Applying the principles in *Full Engagement!* will fundamentally change the performance and culture of any organization. Brian effectively provides actionable tools that get results through an authentic approach that truly engages people the right way."

—Tim Larson, President and CEO, Jostens

"This is an outstanding book, loaded with practical tools and ideas that every manager can use to help employees feel terrific about themselves—and as you know, an engaged, happy employee is the central value in individual performance and productivity. This book shows you how to motivate and inspire your team to achieve their highest potential."

—John Assaraf, author

"Leaders and managers can extract the worst or best of what employees have in them. Now more than ever before we need the best quality work and highest productivity from the employees we have—and nobody is better at showing us how than Brian Tracy."

—Lawrence Janesky, President, Basement Systems Inc.; author, *The Highest Calling* and *Think Daily*

"Brian has done it again! *Full Engagement!* teaches all of us who manage or lead others how to get the most out of those we work with. In this ever-changing world, Brian Tracy provides an easy-to-follow roadmap to peak performance! This book is a 'must' for every leader!"

—Tom Alkazin, Royal Ambassador and Top Earner, Vemma

FULL ENGAGEMENT!

Inspire, Motivate, and
Bring Out the Best in Your People

Brian Tracy

AMACOM

American Management Association
New York • Atlanta • Brussels • Chicago • Mexico City • San Francisco
Shanghai • Tokyo • Toronto • Washington, D.C.

This publication is designed to provide accurate and authoritative information in regard to the subject matter covered. It is sold with the understanding that the publisher is not engaged in rendering legal, accounting, or other professional service. If legal advice or other expert assistance is required, the services of a competent professional person should be sought.

Library of Congress Cataloging-in-Publication Data

Tracy, Brian.
    Full engagement! : inspire, motivate, and bring out the best in your people /
Brian Tracy.
        p.   cm.
    Includes index.
    ISBN-13: 978-0-8144-1689-1
    ISBN-10: 0-8144-1689-6
    1. Employee motivation.   2. Performance.   3. Organizational effectiveness.
4. Organizational behavior.   I. Title.
    HF5549.5.M63T73   2011
    658.3′14—dc22

                                                                    2010048293

About AMA

American Management Association (www.amanet.org) is a world leader in talent development, advancing the skills of individuals to drive business success. Our mission is to support the goals of individuals and organizations through a complete range of products and services, including classroom and virtual seminars, webcasts, webinars, podcasts, conferences, corporate and government solutions, business books and research. AMA's approach to improving performance combines experiential learning—learning through doing—with opportunities for ongoing professional growth at every step of one's career journey.

Printing number

10 9 8 7 6 5 4 3 2 1

This book is fondly dedicated to Art Van Elsander and Kim Yost and the wonderful company they lead. Art Van Furniture represents the very best of modern management today.

Contents

• • • CONTENTS

FULL ENGAGEMENT!

Introduction

"If your actions inspire others to dream more, learn more, do more, and become more, then you are a leader."

—John Quincy Adams

Welcome to the new world of business! We have gone through a watershed in business activities and operations since 2008, and things will never be the same again. What you are dealing with today is the "new normal." The good old days are gone forever.

Because of shrinking markets, increased competition, demanding customers, and a never-ending shortage of highly qualified, productive people, you will have to do more with less, and get better results from limited resources, more than ever before.

One of the interesting outcomes of these challenging economic times is that companies are producing more with fewer resources. They have laid off millions of people and downsized in almost every area. But the level of productivity, performance, and output per person has actually gone up. Companies are maintaining or increasing their levels of productivity and quality with fewer people, but with people who are better selected, better organized, and better managed. This must be your goal as well.

As a manager at any level, you are essentially the operator of your own personal business unit. You have revenues and expenses, inputs and outputs, production requirements and measures of performance. Your profit-and-loss statement reflects your ability to combine people and resources to get results—especially financial results—that are in excess, and, ideally, greatly in excess, of their total costs.

Increasing Your ROE

The measure of *business* success is largely determined by how well the managers of the business achieve a high and consistent return on equity (ROE). The purpose of strategy, planning, tactics, and operations is to organize and reorganize the people and assets of the business in such a way that this return on equity, which is the return on the actual capital that the owners have invested in the business, is the very highest possible in any market, and especially in comparison with competitors in the same business or industry.

As a manager, your job is to achieve the highest ROE as well. Only ROE refers to the "return on energy" of the people who report to you. Your central focus should be to achieve the highest possible return on human capital—the physical, emotional, and mental effort—that your people invest, or are capable of investing, in achieving the results for which you are responsible.

According to Robert Half International, the average person works at about 50 percent of capacity. Because of unclear job assignments, lack of priorities, poor management and direction, and lack of feedback, the average employee wastes 50 percent or more of his time in activities that have nothing to do with the job.

This wasted time is consumed in idle chitchat with co-workers, extended lunches and coffee breaks, employees coming in late and leaving early, surfing the Internet, and engaging in personal business and other time-filling activities that represent virtually no return to the company on the amount of money invested in paying people's salaries, wages, and benefits.

But, as Napoleon said, "There are no bad soldiers under a good general." A good manager with a clear vision can quickly organize a group of average performers into a peak performance team that is capable of achieving tremendous results for the company. You just need to learn how to do it.

The good news is that all the answers have already been found and are readily available. As the result of decades of research and millions of hours invested in personal and organizational performance, we now know exactly what you need to do, and to stop doing, to get the very best out of your people. Since 65 to 85 percent of the cost of operating a business (aside from cost of goods sold) is consumed in salaries and wages, your ability to tap into the unused 50 percent of this investment, owing to employees working at half speed, and channel the human energies of your staff into higher levels of productivity and performance, enables you to make a real difference in your position, whatever it is.

Learning What You Need to Learn

Another thing we know is that every excellent manager today was once a *poor* manager. Everyone starts at the bottom with no managerial skills at all, no matter what a person's title. My personal experience is a good example. I remember when I was first promoted from a top salesman to a sales management position with more than thirty salespeople under me. I was convinced that this was a great opportunity for me to demonstrate my leadership abilities.

Having no management experience, I immediately began giving orders, telling people to do certain things and to stop doing other things. I lectured to both individuals and groups to demonstrate my superior knowledge and competence in our business. I criticized people for mistakes or lack of productivity and threatened to fire people who didn't smarten up and fly right.

I ignored the sullen looks and brooding faces, dismissed the silence that greeted me whenever I walked into the room. I was oblivious to the small groups of salespeople who were joining together and complaining among themselves about my behavior and the way I was treating them.

A week after I was promoted into this management position, I arrived at the office one morning to find it empty. Everyone was gone. They had cleared out as if there had been a bomb scare. The only person left was the secretary, who told me that the top salesman in the company, a man who was very popular and influential among the other salespeople, had quietly organized the group and then made an offer to a competitor to bring the entire sales team over, along with their customers, to sell a similar product for the rival firm. Because of the way I had been treating them, and some peer pressure thrown in, the whole group walked out.

Taking Stock

My reaction was shock and disbelief. I knew that when my boss heard about it, I would be fired and put back out on the street, exactly where I had started some years before.

Not knowing what to do, I called on a wiser, older businessman, told him what had happened, and asked for his advice. Because he had been through a similar situation early in his career, he told me exactly what had happened, the mistakes I had made, and what I needed to do immediately to turn the situation around.

First, I had to be willing to accept that I had personally made a major mistake, and that I was responsible for rectifying it. The next key to solving this problem was the top salesman who had spearheaded the massive defection. If I could get him to come back, before the group had settled into the rival company, I could turn the situation around.

Making Up

His name was Phillip. I called him right away and arranged a meeting. He showed up with three other top salespeople, like a mafia sit-down, and asked me what I wanted. I immediately apologized for my behavior, promised never to treat the salespeople poorly again, and asked him what it would take to get him to come back. After some private conversation with his *consiglieres*, he told me what I would have to do.

His demands were simple. I would appoint him assistant sales manager and work through him as a liaison to the entire sales force. I would henceforth treat each person with respect, and if I had problems, talk with him before criticizing or complaining in public. I agreed, and the next day the entire sales team reappeared at the office, ready to work.

From that learning experience, I went on to build sales forces in six countries, recruiting, training, staffing, then appointing managers and helping them to manage their operations successfully. Each of the sales teams was soon producing excellent results for the company. I had learned a valuable lesson and I never forgot it.

The Heart of the Matter

Here's the lesson: The way you treat people, what you say and do that affects them *emotionally*, is more important in bringing out the best in people than all the education, intelligence, or experience you might have at doing your job. The best news of all is that because you are motivated and influenced by the same things other people are, you already know everything you need to know to become an outstanding manager. You already know how to unlock the potential of the people around you, how to build a peak performance team that delivers consistently high levels of results for your company. You just need to apply it.

In the pages ahead, you will learn, or be reminded, how to get the best out of almost every person who reports to you. At the same time, you will learn why *you* think and feel the way you do about yourself and your work and, by extension, why other people think, feel, react, and respond the way they do at work. You will learn how to use the "boomerang effect," doing and saying those very things that make people feel great about themselves and, as a consequence, make you feel happy about yourself.

Peter Drucker once said that the most important shift you can make in your vocabulary in business is to use the word *contribution* instead of *success*. When you start thinking in terms of contribution, your whole attitude about yourself, as a manager, and other people in the workplace as well, changes in a very positive way.

Why Synergy Is the Key

The greatest contribution you can make to your company is to get the very best out of the human assets entrusted to you. This requires synergy. The word *synergy* refers to the ability of a group of people, working together in harmony, to achieve vastly more than the total work output of the individuals added together. It is said that "no one is as good alone as we are all together."

When people synergize, the output of four people becomes the output of six or seven. The output of eight or ten people can become the output of fifteen or twenty. In this sense, your job is to be a "multiplier." When your personality, talents, and skills are multiplied by any group of people, the output and results achieved should be vastly greater than the addition of one more person. Your job is to be the catalyst that activates and motivates higher levels of performance than would have occurred in your absence.

The 80/20 Rule Revisited

One of the persistent questions in business has always been, "Why are some companies more successful and profitable than others?"

Why do 20 percent of companies earn 80 percent of the profits in each industry? Why do 20 percent of companies enjoy 80 percent of the growth in any particular industry? Why do 20 percent of companies sell 80 percent of the products and the services sold in any market? Why is it that some companies are more successful than others?

The answer is simple: The best companies have the *best managers.* As a result, the best companies have the best people, and that means people who consistently outthink, outcompete, and outperform their competitors.

The true measure of your value as an executive is *performance.* It is your ability to get the most important results that are expected of you. Like a craftsman, your tools are the people with whom you have to work. All work is done by *teams,* and the quality of the team is determined by the performance of the individual team members. Your ability to get the best out of each person largely determines your results, your rewards, your income, your rate of promotion, and your ultimate level of success in your business.

There are two simple rules for success as a manager: Rule number one says, "Your life only gets better when you get better." Rule number two: "Your people only get better when you get better."

Since there is no limit to how much better you can get in the weeks and months ahead, there is no real limit to how good a manager you can become, or to the quantity and quality of the results you can achieve in your position.

So, as you progress through this book, get ready to learn practical, proven strategies for unleashing the potential of your staff, significantly increasing your results and rewards, and becoming an excellent manager for the rest of your career.

CHAPTER ONE

Happy for Good Reasons

"Create the highest, grandest vision possible for your life,
because you become what you believe."

—OPRAH WINFREY

In my sales and marketing classes, I often ask the partici-
pants, "What percentage of human decision making is ratio-
nal and what percentage is emotional?"

Most people answer "80/20" or "90/10." I then complete
the exercise by pointing out that people are 100 percent emotional. Human beings, including yourself, decide *emotionally*
and then justify logically. We make emotional decisions instantaneously, sometimes with a single glance or a single
piece of information, and then we often spend several hours
or months underpinning our emotional decision with logical
justifications.

I then ask, "What is the basic emotional drive behind all human action and behavior?"

After a few random answers such as "money," or "fear of loss," "desire for gain," or even "love," everyone finally agrees that the most powerful single motivator is the "desire to be happy."

Aristotle talked about this in his work *Nichomachean Ethics*. He said that behind every human motive there is a further motive until you finally arrive at the basic motive for everything, and that is to be happy.

Happy Customers

The reason that people buy things is that they feel that they will be happier after buying the item than they were before. People buy in anticipation of how they think they will *feel* as the result of the buying decision. The goal of the salesperson or marketer is to sell "hope." It is the hope of greater happiness rather than lesser happiness that causes every human action, including buying decisions.

The most important question in business is: "If the purpose of a business is to *create and keep a customer,* what is the most important goal you must achieve with each customer if you want the person to buy and buy again?"

And the answer is simple: Make the customer happy that he did business with you. Make the customer *happier* doing business with you, from the beginning of the buying experience through to the customer service experience afterward, than he would be if he had bought from someone else. Happiness is the key.

Happy Employees

The logical extension of this line of questioning for managers is: "How do you get the best out of each person who reports to you?"

How do you get people to willingly contribute their highest levels of physical, emotional, and mental energies to you, and to do their jobs in the very best way possible? How do you get people to be committed, loyal, and dedicated to you and the company? How do you get people to work together harmoniously and continually seek ways to do their jobs better and faster, and at lower cost?

And the answer is, *Make them feel happy.* Organize the work, from the first step in the hiring process through to the final step in the retirement ceremony, so that people are happy with you, their work, their coworkers, as well as in their interactions with your customers, suppliers, and vendors, and in everything they do that has an effect on your company.

Throughout the centuries, wise men, researchers, and scientists of all kinds have sought a "unified field theory," a single umbrellalike principle that explains all other principles. Einstein's formulation of the general theory of relativity ($E = mc^2$) was the breakthrough theory that superseded Newtonian physics at the beginning of the twentieth century, and it is still being applied and expanded upon today as others continue the search for the unified field theory of physics.

In the area of management and motivation, "make them feel happy" is the unified field theory, the principle that explains all other principles.

Practicing Golden Rule Management

Fortunately, "make them feel happy" is both simple and easy to do. All that is necessary is for you to practice the Golden Rule in all of your actions: "Do unto others as you would have them do unto you." It has been said that there are many ideas for improving human relations that have been discovered over the centuries, but nothing has yet been discovered that is superior to this simple principle. In fact, it is the underlying principle or rule of most of the world's great religions.

The challenge has nothing to do with not *knowing* what to do to make people feel happy at their work. Everyone knows *exactly* what to do. The problem is that we either forget to do those things that make people happy, neglect to do them because we are distracted by other things, refuse to do them because we don't understand their importance, or, worst of all, do things that actually make people unhappy and then justify our behavior with self-righteous excuses and rationalizations.

The starting point is learning why and how people think and act the way they do. Then you will understand how to get your people fully engaged in their jobs and how to get the most important results that your business depends upon for success in an increasingly competitive marketplace. You will also learn how your own personality has developed to this day, how to create a peak performance workplace, how to practice "motivational management," and how to get the very most and best out of yourself in everything you do.

A Crash Course in Happiness

Because you are reading this book, you are probably overwhelmed with having too much to do in too little time. Many readers of business books seldom get past the first chapter. For that reason, I am going to give you a "crash course" in this first chapter in making people happy so that they perform at their best.

Here are twenty-five ideas, not necessarily in order, that you can apply to create a peak performance work environment and to ensure that each person makes a maximum contribution to your company. In the pages ahead, I will expand on these ideas and go into some of them in greater depth. But here is where you can start, right now:

1. *Smile.* When you see someone for the first time each day, smile at that person. Look people square in the face, pause, and smile, making it clear that you are happy to see them. It takes just 13 muscles to smile and 112 muscles to frown. So it is much easier to smile at people when you see them each day. And it makes them happy.

2. *Ask people questions.* Talk to them; ask them questions about how they are feeling today and how everything is going. When you express a genuine interest in other people, it makes them feel valuable, respected, and important. They'll feel good inside and want to please you by doing a good job.

3. *Listen to them.* Listen attentively when people talk to you. When you listen to people closely, without interruption, it makes them feel valuable and important. It raises their self-esteem. Being intensely listened to by the boss actually releases endorphins in people's brains, which causes them to feel happier and better about themselves. When you listen, nod, smile, and watch the person's face intently. Show that you are treating the person as though what she is saying is of great interest and importance to you. Active listening only takes a few moments each day, but it has a powerful, positive effect on how other people do their jobs.

4. *Be polite.* Always be polite, courteous, and respectful when you talk with your staff members. Treat them as if they are talented, intelligent, and accomplished. Lean forward and face them directly, as if there is nothing else in the world that you would rather do than interact with them at this moment.

5. *Say "thank you."* For everything they do, small or large, thank people. Thank them for being at the meeting on time,

for completing an assignment, for giving you a piece of information, and for any other thing that they do that is part of their job. When you express appreciation toward other people, thanking them for something they have done or said, you make them feel more valuable and important. Because your words have a powerful impact on their thoughts, feelings, and behavior, when you thank people, you make them feel happier about themselves and their work.

6. *Keep people informed.* Keep them fully informed about the company, the business, and especially anything that is going on that may have an impact on their work or their security in their job. The most satisfied employees in every organization report that they feel that they are insiders, that they are "in the know," and that they are aware of everything that is going on around them that affects them or their work in any way.

It helps to practice an open-door policy. Tell people that there are "no secrets" and that if anyone ever has any questions about anything that is going on inside or outside the business, they are free to ask and their questions will be answered.

7. *Encourage improvement.* Encourage people to come up with ideas to do their jobs better or to improve the company in any way possible. The Japanese rebuilt their economy after World War II with the *kaizen* system, which stands for "continuous betterment." They encouraged every person, at every level, to look for small and large improvements that they could make in their "line of sight."

You should do the same. When someone comes up with an idea, no matter what you might think of it initially, encourage the person to try it out on a small scale to see if it works.

The more ideas you encourage, the more ideas you are going to get. And when people are encouraged to use their creativity to do their job better, they feel much happier about themselves and the company.

8. *Treat your employees like volunteers.* Treat them as if they were working for free. Imagine that each member of your staff is a talented, accomplished person who could work anywhere she wants but has chosen to work for you because she likes you and the company.

In nonprofit organizations, where almost everyone is a volunteer, each person who comes to help out in organizational activities is treated with tremendous respect because the managers want those people to come back and help out in the future. When you treat your staff as if they were unpaid volunteers, donating their time to help you and the business because they like you and enjoy what they are doing, you will treat them better. This will cause them to feel much happier about coming to work and doing their jobs.

9. *Imagine your employees as million-dollar customers.* Think about how your personality changes when you hear the voice of one of your important customers on the phone. You instantly become warm, friendly, charming, attentive, and respective. You are on your very best behavior. No matter what the customer says, you remain thoughtful, patient, friendly, and agreeable.

Now, imagine that each of your employees is in a position to influence a million-dollar purchase of your products or services in some way. When you treat each of your staff members the same way you would treat one of your most valuable customers, it has an enormous positive effect on them and makes them feel very good about themselves and about working for you.

10. *Pay people well.* Reward them fairly and pay them well for the contribution they make. Although money itself is not a major motivator, being paid less than a person is actually worth is a major demotivator.

The fact is that all good people are free, since good people contribute more value to the company than they cost in salaries and benefits. Companies can only grow to the degree to which they can attract and keep excellent people whose work continually increases the bottom line.

When you consider that longer-term employees have built up an enormous stock of intellectual capital about your company, the job they do and how to do it well, and the various people that they work with both inside and outside the company, you become aware of how difficult and expensive it is to replace good people.

When in doubt, pay people more rather than less. Offer to increase their pay instead of waiting for them to come to you and ask for a raise. Tell them how much you value their work and their contribution and back it up financially. This way you'll make people feel valuable and important, and more loyal to you and the business.

11. *Compliment people.* Take time to admire their possessions, appearance, and qualities or traits. Everyone likes a compliment. You can compliment someone on an article of clothing, a new purse or briefcase, or even a haircut or change in hairstyle. In addition, you can compliment people on their qualities or traits. "You are very persistent," or "You always do an excellent job."

People invest a lot of time and emotion in their personal appearance, their homes, their cars, their accomplishments, and their behaviors. When you take a minute to notice and comment positively on any one of these areas, you make people feel valuable and special and happier about themselves and what they are doing.

12. *Assure harmony.* You want your people working with other positive, competent people. One of your most important jobs as the leader is to make sure that everyone is working in a positive climate of harmony and happiness.

One negative or difficult person can poison the entire work environment. Your job is to make sure that people are happy when they work with their coworkers, and to take whatever steps are necessary to encourage negative, difficult people to go and work somewhere else.

13. *Praise them regularly.* Give your employees praise and approval for every accomplishment, both large and small. One of the definitions of self-esteem is the degree to which a person feels "praiseworthy."

Whenever you praise other people for anything, you immediately raise their self-esteem and make them feel more valuable and important. When people feel good about themselves because of your praise, they become internally motivated to repeat the behavior or performance that earned your praise in the first place. As a result, they do more and more important things, and get better and better at them each time.

The rules for praise are simple: First, praise *immediately.* Praise people right after they have done something worthwhile or completed a task. The faster the praise, the greater its impact.

Second, praise *specifically.* Mention the exact job or accomplishment that the person has completed and talk about the specific measure or task that has been done so well. The more specific your praise, the easier it is for people to repeat that behavior in the future.

Third, praise *publicly* whenever possible. Whenever you praise a person in front of one or more other people, the power of the praise in influencing her behavior is multiplied by the number of people who hear the praise.

All good managers continually seek out opportunities and places to praise people in front of others for their accomplishments. This is something only the manager can do, and when done consistently and well, it makes people feel terrific about themselves and about working for you.

14. *Don't criticize.* Refuse to criticize, condemn, or complain about anyone or anything within earshot of your staff. Negativity of any kind, no matter how justified, demoralizes people and makes them feel insecure and unhappy.

If you have a problem, keep it to yourself. If you have a difficult situation, you can explain to others what has happened objectively and unemotionally. Then, ask if anyone has any ideas on steps or actions that you could take to solve the problem or resolve the difficulty.

There is nothing wrong with having problems, difficulties, obstacles, setbacks, and adversity in the world of work. They happen every single day. The only real question is how you respond to these challenges. Resolve that no matter what happens, you will focus on the future and on the solution. You will concentrate on what can be done now, rather than what has happened in the past. You will keep yourself, and everyone else, thinking about creative ways to overcome obstacles and achieve goals.

15. *Celebrate success.* On a regular basis, you want to celebrate the successes both of individuals and of the team as a whole. Bring in lunch from outside for everyone to celebrate an accomplishment, such as signing a major contract, or just as a way to express your appreciation for the good job that

everyone is doing. For more significant achievements, you can take your team out to lunch at a local restaurant. At your regular staff meetings, you can start off by singling out one or more people who have accomplished something noteworthy, then lead a round of applause for those people in front of everyone else.

Whenever you celebrate someone's accomplishment, that person is doubly motivated to do it again, and everyone else in attendance is motivated to perhaps do something that will earn them the same kind of celebration.

16. *Express interest in people.* Take an interest in their personal lives. Ask them about their families, their relationships, what sort of things they do when they are not at work, and how things are going in general. The fact is that every person has a complex, busy, emotionally charged, and active life away from the office. For most people, their personal lives are the centerpieces of almost everything they think or feel, and their work life is secondary.

When you take a genuine interest in people, and see them as individuals rather than just as coworkers, they feel more valuable and important. The very fact that you are interested in them makes them happy.

17. *Be a mentor.* Look for ways to guide people to learn, grow, and improve in what they do. Suggest books and articles, and even buy them for your staff. Encourage them to take additional seminars and courses, and offer to pay for them. Give your employees time off for continuous personal and professional development.

One of the greatest desires that each person has is to learn, grow, and become more valuable. In your position as manager, you have learned an enormous amount about what subjects your employees need to master in order to become more valuable to themselves and to their business.

Some managers ask, "What if we train them and they leave?" But that is the wrong question. The right question is, "What if we *don't* train them, and they stay?"

The more time you take to mentor your staff, to give them guidance and advice, and to encourage them to learn and grow, the better they feel about themselves, and the more likely they are to stay with you for a long time.

18. *Set them free.* Give the people on your staff freedom to do their work. People like to know exactly what it is that you want them to do, but they should also be given as much freedom as possible to do the job in their own way.

Encourage people to accept a high level of responsibility for their work, and for the way they organize themselves and use their time. As people demonstrate that they are self-reliant and self-directed, give them more and more freedom to do their jobs in the best way that they know how. The more freedom that people feel they have, within clear boundaries, the happier they are about themselves and their work, and the better work they do.

19. *Protect them.* Protect them from the negativity, rudeness, or bad treatment of other people, both inside and outside the company. This is very important. You must never allow anyone to verbally mistreat a member of your staff, just as you would not allow a person to mistreat a member of your family.

If someone inside your company mistreats a member of your staff, you should address it immediately and insist that it not happen again. If someone from outside of your company, even a customer, is rude or abusive to a member of your staff, you should deal with it immediately and make sure that it doesn't happen again.

When your staff members know that you will stand up for

them and protect them from the negative words or behaviors of others, they feel safer, more secure, and happier in their work. This is absolutely essential for top performance.

20. *See them as your children.* When you really love and care for your children, you are patient with them as they go through the learning curve. The fact is that "adults are just children with better excuses." No matter how old we grow, we still think and act like children in many ways. When you practice patience, compassion, and tolerance with your staff, just as you would with your younger children as they are growing up, your entire attitude and behavior will be different.

When you are raising your children, you think long term about your behaviors toward them. You realize that the ups and downs they experience as they are growing up are insignificant in the greater context of the people they become as adults. Therefore, you don't overreact when they do or say something inappropriate. After all, they are only children.

When you extend this way of thinking toward your staff, being nonjudgmental, patient and accepting, and completely supportive of them, you create a safe environment where people feel motivated to express themselves fully and do the very best they can.

21. *Be pleasant and agreeable.* Resolve to be pleasant, positive, and agreeable with each person on your staff. Treat people in a warm and friendly way. Always be cheerful and optimistic.

The emotional tone of the manager sets the emotional tone for the entire staff. People are very sensitive to the thoughts, feelings, and behaviors of the person who controls their job and their paycheck. When you are positive and cheerful, you create a safe environment where others are positive and cheerful as well. If you are upset or angry, your emotions and attitudes immediately exert a negative effect on everyone around you.

One of the most important responsibilities you have as a manager is to create an environment within which people feel happy, positive, secure, and valuable. You create this environment with every word you say, every glance you cast, and every response you give to the various activities that are going on around you.

Top executives always think in terms of the potential *consequences* of their behaviors. Rather than giving in to short-term anger or irritation, they practice self-control. They reflect on how their behavior is likely to affect the thoughts, feelings, and behaviors of others, and they then act accordingly.

22. *Build them up.* Speak positively about your staff to other people. Brag about the members of your staff on every occasion. Speak glowingly about individuals on your staff to *other* individuals on your staff.

Because you are the boss, everything you say will be repeated and passed on to others. Whenever you say something nice about someone, your words will get back to that person almost instantaneously, and in a very positive way.

By the same token, if you say anything negative about anyone at any time, for any reason, your words will get back to that person, and what you said will be multiplied out of all proportion in a completely distorted and negative way. Be careful.

23. *Be clear about what their jobs entail.* Be sure each person knows exactly what they are expected to do, how it will be measured, and when it is due. One of the greatest gifts that you can give your staff (something I'll talk about more in

subsequent chapters) is *clarity.* The greater clarity people have about what you want them to do, and how it will be measured, the easier it is for them to throw their whole hearts into doing an excellent job. And it is only when people put their whole hearts into their work that they feel truly happy about themselves and what they are doing.

24. *Give feedback.* Give your staff regular feedback, advice, and guidance about the work and how they are doing their jobs. The more feedback you give, the better the people on your staff will feel about themselves, and about doing the job even better in the future.

Taking the time to sit down and chat with your coworkers about what they are doing and how it is going often presents opportunities to solve problems, give guidance, and ensure that the individual does the very best job possible. When people know what they are supposed to do, and get regular feedback from their bosses, they feel valuable and happy about themselves.

25. *Treat your staff like you treat your boss.* Treat each person as though she was going to be promoted and become your boss in the next couple of months, and imagine only you know about this impending decision. When you think about working under the person who is now working under you, it changes the way you treat that person in a very positive way. You become far more positive, thoughtful, balanced, and constructive in all of your interactions. You become more polite, courteous, and respectful to that person if that person is going to be your boss in a short time.

When you use this way of thinking as your guide for the way you treat your coworkers, you will be amazed at how much more effective you are, and how much better the results your team achieves are.

As you can see, each of these twenty-five recommendations requires little more than a shift in attitude and behavior on your part. You don't have to change your entire personality or become a completely different person. To make people feel really happy about themselves and their work, you simply have to treat them exactly the way you would like to be treated, over and over again, until it becomes a series of automatic and easy behaviors for you.

In its simplest terms, you can measure your success as a manager, the productivity of your area of responsibility, and the future of your business by ranking each person on a scale from 1 to 10, from very unhappy to very happy.

Think about it. How would you rank each of your staff members on this scale? Even better, go and ask them how they would rank themselves in terms of how happy they are today. Then ask everyone, "What would have to happen for you to be happier in the future?"

Four Ways to Change

There are only four ways that you can change anything about yourself, your life, your work, or your relationships with others:

1. You can do *more* of certain things. What should you be doing more of to build a positive, upbeat, happy work environment?

2. You could do *less* of other things. What should you be doing less of if you want people to feel wonderful about themselves every day?

3. You could *start* doing something that you are not doing today. What things should you start doing that would cause people to feel happier about themselves and their work?

(Start with any of the twenty-five items described in this chapter.)

4. You could *stop* certain behaviors altogether. What are the things that you are doing on a regular basis that you should discontinue?

If you are not sure about any of the answers to these questions, sit down with your staff, as individuals or in a group setting, and have the courage and honesty to ask them these questions: What would you like me to do more of in the days and weeks ahead? What would you like me to do less of? What would you like me to start doing that I am not doing today? What would you like me to stop doing altogether?

Getting Started by Working on a Single Behavior

Keep notes, and then select *one behavior* that seems to be of great importance to other people and begin working on that single behavior every single day. Keep at it until you master that behavior and then make it a permanent part of your personality. It may take a week, a month, or a year, but the payoff will be extraordinary. By developing one specific positive, constructive behavioral attribute, you can often bring about a transformation of your workplace, unleash the potential of your staff as never before, and become an extraordinary manager for the months and years ahead.

Action Exercises

1. Identify one behavior that you could practice that would make your company a happier place to work.

2. Resolve to greet and speak to each of your staff members every day as early as possible.

3. Look for opportunities to praise people for good work that they are doing.

4. Listen attentively to people when they speak to you, either alone or in a group.

5. Treat each person as if he was vital to your business and was thinking of taking another job where he would be more appreciated.

6. Talk to people as if any one of them was going to be your boss and determine your income and duties one month from today.

7. Ask people regularly if there is anything you could do to make their job easier.

CHAPTER TWO

The Psychology of Motivation

"The only certain means of success is to render
more and better service than is expected of you,
no matter what your task may be."

—OG MANDINO, AUTHOR

Some years ago, when I was doing some speaking and training work for Hewlett-Packard, I learned of a division of the company that was run by the best managers in the company's history. People loved the company and their work so much that they stayed and worked hours into the evening, even after they had caught up and could quite comfortably have gone home.

It reached the point where the security guards would have to go through the building and shut off the power to get people to go home at ten and eleven o'clock at night. Then, the employees began coming back on the weekends so that they could be at the office with their coworkers and put in even more hours. It reached the point where HP had to hire security guards to stop people from getting into the building on the weekends to continue working because they enjoyed their work so much. They had to be forced to take time off with their families and for their personal lives. What a story!

Your ability to create an environment where your people feel fully engaged with their jobs and the company is essential for you to get the best out of others. Because each person is different from everyone else, complex in many ways, and possessing a variety of hopes, fears, dreams, ambitions, and motivations, getting people engaged is not simple, but it is eminently achievable.

When I was growing up, almost everyone drove a stick shift, a car where you had to shift through first, second, and third gears to reach top speed. When the car was driven properly, the gears would mesh smoothly, quietly, and efficiently from one speed to the next. When the car was driven poorly, or had an older transmission, the gears would often clash. The sound they made was awful, and it required immediate attention to get the gears humming along and working smoothly once more. A good driver could actually shift gears without even touching the clutch, just by increasing and decreasing the speed as he went from one gear to the next.

There is a definite parallel to this concept in getting the best out of others. An excellent manager, like a good driver, can shift the gears of power, influence, and control smoothly, from person to person, melding people into a team of high performers with little or no grinding or clashing of gears. Everyone works smoothly and efficiently together to get the job done and move the company forward. This is your goal.

Starting with Yourself

The starting point in getting the most out of others is to understand *yourself* and what motivates you to do your best. The starting point of understanding yourself is for you to thoroughly understand some of the great breakthroughs in motivational psychology that have taken place in the last hundred years.

The only real test for truth is contained in the question: "Is this true for me?" As you learn about how to motivate others, ask if these ideas are true for you as well. The first part of "motivation" is the word *motive*. Do the same motives that cause other people to act cause you to act as well? When you can see the clear link between what motivates you and what motivates others, you are able to learn, internalize, and practice these principles much faster than if you just think about them as tools you can use to get the best out of others.

One of the best ways to learn and internalize any subject is to practice "dual-plane learning." That is, while you are learning a subject, you consciously decide to learn it on two levels. You think about how the principles apply to other people, and at the same time how these principles apply to you, your life, and your own personal experiences.

You only really understand a new subject, such as motivational psychology, when you put yourself into the picture. You need to understand the principles of motivation in terms of how they apply to you, and how they have affected your thoughts, feelings, and behaviors in the past.

Each person is unique and different in countless ways. But each person is similar to others in many other ways as well. To be an effective executive, you need a clear understanding of why people do the things they do, and what you can change in yourself and in the work environment to enable people to perform at the highest levels possible.

Scientific Management

At the beginning of the twentieth century, the vast majority of industrial workers in the United States were unskilled laborers who left the farms and moved to the cities, just as they had done during the Industrial Revolution in England, starting in 1815. At this time, when large industrial organizations were forming for the first time, Frederick Taylor's "scientific management" method was the predominant influence in the management and organization of human resources. Taylor taught that each job or series of jobs could be broken down into individual components. By assigning workers to each component—a process known as the "specialization of labor"—average semiskilled and unskilled laborers could be organized into efficient work groups that produced complex products, such as automobiles and appliances.

Taylor also emphasized the importance of "time and motion studies," which identified the very best way to perform manufacturing functions and the optimum amount of time that should be spent on that function. By applying Taylor's principles to manufacturing, thousands of men and women could be organized into huge groups in large factories to produce enormous quantities of products at continually lower prices, with no loss of quality.

One of the challenges of scientific management was that it relied totally on *external* decisions, *external* organization, and *external* supervision. Workers were largely considered to be interchangeable, so they could be moved around from job to job, at will, by the foreman, supervisor, and manager.

Behaviorism Becomes Popular

The standardization and homogenization of workers led to B. F. Skinner's influential breakthroughs in motivational psychology that went under the name of "behaviorism." Individuals were largely considered to be organisms that could be motivated or discouraged by rewards and punishments. If you wanted them to do something, such as to work productively with others to produce products in factories, you merely had to raise the reward level to get them to do it, or raise the punishment level for not doing it the way you wanted them to. These methods are still common in child rearing today and in the modern workplace.

As a result of standardizing the work process, large numbers of people could be organized, productivity could be increased, quality could be maintained or increased, and prices could be lowered—and, as a consequence, manufactured products such as automobiles could be made available to the average working person for the first time.

Routine Work Is Boring

The downside of the standardization of labor and scientific management was that the jobs became increasingly simple and incredibly *boring*. Working on a production line, hour after hour, and earning a steady salary was ideal for people who had just moved to the city. But after a few years, the stultifying boredom became too much. Workers became disaffected. The union movement emerged to capture and channel this disaffection into industrial action. Labor–management conflicts broke out between the people who owned and managed the factories and the people who worked there.

To a greater or lesser degree, the standardization of labor in large industrial installations, combined with the increasing boredom of the work, led to shutdowns, strikes, lockouts, industrial actions, and the growth of a powerful union movement to defend the unhappy worker in contract negotiations against the factory owner or employer. This story line continued right up to the 1950s when, as the result of increasingly complex "knowledge work" and higher levels of education among the American workforce, workers and employees became far more individualistic, demanding, and selective about the work they would do and the conditions under which they would do it. It was at this time that one of the great breakthroughs in motivational psychology began to be applied to an ever-expanding workforce.

The Hawthorne Experiments

This breakthrough in the understanding of individual motivation took place in 1928 at the Hawthorne Works, a Western Electric plant just outside of Chicago. Following Frederick Taylor's principles of scientific management, a group of human resources specialists decided to experiment with different ways to increase the productivity of women assembling electric motors. They reviewed the personnel records of the women in the plant, several hundred of them, and selected a small group to be the subjects of this research. They told the women that they had been selected for this research because of their excellent work records. The researchers explained that they were going to be looking for ways to increase productivity and output in the plant, and would be changing different factors in the work environment to observe those factors that seemed to have the greatest impact on productivity levels.

No Clear Explanation

Over the next few weeks, they began their experiments by raising the light levels in the special assembly area. Not unsurprisingly, productivity levels went up as the light levels were raised. Then, they *lowered* the light levels. To their surprise, productivity levels increased again over the daily average.

This seemingly inexplicable phenomenon occurred when they raised and lowered the temperature, raised and lowered noise levels, raised and then lowered the air-conditioning and the factory's ambient odors. In every case, with every change, productivity levels improved.

By the end of the experiment, the researchers were beside themselves. They could not decipher the data in any meaningful way. Finally, one of them said, "Why don't we ask the women workers if they have any insights into these production levels?"

An Incredible Breakthrough

The researchers brought the women in, sat them down, and explained what they had done and the results that they had gotten from the experiment. They explained that no matter what they had done, production levels went up. This outcome did not fit any of the explanations based on scientific management.

After some discussion and questioning, the women finally made an admission that explained why production levels had gone up. It was simple: The women said that when they had been selected from the workforce in the plant for this experiment, they had felt "special." They felt that they were highly appreciated and valued by the plant's management. Not only that, their other coworkers, who had not been selected, looked upon them as being somehow superior to the average plant employee.

As a result, whenever the experimenters changed some factor in the workplace, it *reminded* them that they were special, different, and more highly productive. As a result, they worked longer, harder, and better. They dedicated themselves to doing a better job and to constantly look for ways to improve.

The researchers eventually dubbed this the "X factor." Later, it became known as the "psychological factor." They concluded that tapping into the thoughts, feelings, and emotions of the workers had a far greater power to motivate higher levels of production than any physical change in factory or work conditions. Is this true for you?

Paying Attention Improves Results

In 1932, German physicist Werner Heisenberg received the Nobel Prize for his work on "the uncertainty principle." The first part of this principle said that physics and mathematics could determine how a certain percentage of molecules in any system would act or react under certain conditions. But neither physics nor mathematics could predict exactly *which* molecules would react in a particular way. Therefore, there was always a high degree of uncertainty in any mathematical or physical formula, no matter how accurate it might otherwise be.

The uncertainty principle is used extensively in our society, especially in the area of insurance of all kinds. Actuarial tables tell us that a certain number of people of a certain age will die in a certain way in any given year. But because we do not know exactly who those people will be, we provide life, medical, and disability insurance to reduce the effects of this "uncertainty."

The second part of Werner Heisenberg's uncertainty principle was his conclusion that the very act of observing a specific activity in science changes the perspective of the researcher, creating uncertainty as to whether the experiment was truly neutral and unbiased.

Here is a simple example: Suppose you tell one of your employees that you are writing a report for senior management on the way people use their time in your department. And then you tell this employee that you have selected him as the one you are going to observe for a week before writing your report. How do you think that person will use his time?

If someone knew that his boss was going to be watching him out of the corner of his eye and observing how he used his time throughout the week, he would of course use his time far more efficiently, especially when the boss was around. The results of this research into how the employee spends work time would be greatly influenced by the degree to which it was observed. The uncertainty principle strikes again!

The experiments at the Western Electric Hawthorne plant also demonstrated that the very act of observing people doing their work, and their knowing that they were being observed, changes their performance, behavior, and productivity. When people are more alert to and aware of what they are doing, rather than simply going through the motions in a routine fashion, they do their work better, make fewer mistakes, and produce more.

Most world records in sports take place in front of large public audiences. The more people there are watching and cheering for the athlete, the better the performance of that athlete. Entertainers usually give their best performances in front of large appreciative audiences. The very act of observing a person doing something changes the way that person does that job or performs that act.

The Postwar Age

After the depressions of the 1930s and World War II, the United States was the "last man standing" among the industrial powers. In the postwar years, there was enormous pent-up demand for every type of consumer product, from automobiles to houses, from clothing to new household appliances. Competition exploded. The unemployed workforce from the 1930s disappeared and labor actually became a scarce commodity. Under the G.I. Bill, millions of young people began pouring out of the universities with higher levels of education, skill, and knowledge and with more demanding consumer appetites. The number of products and services available to them also increased dramatically. In 1950, the average supermarket had fewer than 5,000 items available. By 1965, the average supermarket had more than 50,000 items available in store. Today, it is 100,000 items or more. Companies have had to become more creative and innovative in order to respond quickly to changes in customer demands and to satisfy the needs of consumers who are more highly educated.

The Age of the Knowledge Worker

The age of the "knowledge worker" had begun. The more talented a person, the more job options and opportunities were available to him. The most valuable and productive employees could leave work at any time and walk across the street to a competitor. As a result, the old command-and-control method of management stopped working. To hire and keep good people, from the 1960s on, companies had to provide a working environment where people were happy and dedicated and allowed to use more and more of their mental, physical, and emotional resources and abilities.

The Great Breakthrough

In 1947, Abraham Maslow turned the study of psychology upside down. From the days of Sigmund Freud in 1895 Vienna, psychologists and psychiatrists had studied men and women in an attempt to diagnose and determine the causes of these various forms of unhappiness and dysfunction. By the first half of the twentieth century, there were any number of ideas, theories, and explanations for various psychological problems, and an entire field of psychiatrists, psychologists, psychotherapists, and counselors emerged to help people deal with situations that were making them unhappy and disrupting their quality of life and relationships.

But psychologist Abraham Maslow did the *opposite*. Instead of analyzing unhappy people, he began studying healthy, happy people. He developed extensive survey forms that he gave to individuals and to people who worked with and around those individuals. His goal was to identify people who were experiencing high levels of happiness and fulfillment in most areas of their lives. He then developed what came to be known as "Maslow's hierarchy" of motivation, which is still relevant and applicable today.

What Maslow found was that all people, no matter their individual differences, had specific motivational needs, starting from the most basic and rising to the most complex. His breakthrough was his discovery that each level of need had to be fulfilled to a certain extent before the next higher level need became a motivator. Maslow's hierarchy applies to you and me, and to everyone we work with and who works for us.

The first three needs that Maslow identified are what he called "deficiency needs." If a person feels deficient in one or more of these needs, he becomes preoccupied with satisfying this need to a minimum level before he can think clearly about striving toward something higher or better. Here, then, are the needs that Maslow identified:

1. *Survival.* The most basic need of all creatures, including human beings, is for physical survival. It is to preserve one's life, to have sufficient food and shelter so that one does not fear for his life.

Until this need is satisfied, it blots out all other concerns or considerations. For example, you could be leading a normal, comfortable life and then, while driving home one evening, you get into an accident where your car is forced off the road and flipped over into a river. At that moment, every other thought or consideration in your life will be forgotten. You will only have one motivation, and that is to save your life in some way.

You see the survival instinct at work in wars, revolutions, and tsunamis, when large numbers of people panic and run frantically away from the perceived danger. The only thought they have is to survive.

Fortunately, in our society, survival needs are largely satisfied, except in accidents and other extreme situations. According to the studies, no one has died of starvation in the United States since 1732, except in strange or unpredictable situations. Our society is wealthy enough, and supports so many charities, both public and private, that no one is in danger of losing their life because of poverty or illness. This need is therefore largely satisfied and is not much of a motivator.

This tends to be true in all advanced countries where prosperity has created sufficient resources to provide for those who cannot provide for themselves.

2. *Security.* Once survival needs are satisfied, the individual immediately moves up the hierarchy to the second deficiency need, that of security. Security refers to physical, financial, and emotional security. To feel physically secure, a person needs a home or a place to sleep, clothes to wear, food to eat, and sufficient physical resources so that she does not have to worry about her safety.

To satisfy the needs for financial security, a person has to have enough money so that he can provide for himself and his family. Today, the greatest single fear that adults have is that of poverty or destitution. It is the fear of the loss of their money. Sometimes, this fear is so great that people will actually commit suicide upon learning that they have lost all their money. This basic fear lies at the root of many of our political and social problems today.

To satisfy the needs for emotional security, the individual needs to feel safe in her primary relationships. She needs to feel accepted, respected, and valued at work and at home. If this need is not fulfilled, she will become preoccupied with satisfying it in some way.

3. *Belongingness.* Man is a social animal. Each of us has an identity that is largely shaped by the people around us, starting in infancy and early childhood. All people need to know that they are safe, secure, and accepted by others, both in society at large and in the workplace.

Because how we think and feel about ourselves is largely determined by the way we think *other* people think and feel about us, an individual can suffer extraordinary anxiety and stress if he is rejected by the people in his environment, especially at work. As mentioned previously, one of the most important things you, as a manager, do to create a high-performance employee is to structure a high-performance environment around that person. When people feel accepted, valuable, and important in their work environment, when they feel they are part of something bigger than themselves, this need for belongingness is satisfied. At that point, the individual is then free to turn his time and attention to higher things, like productivity, performance, and making a valuable contribution to the company.

In the work world, we satisfy the three basic needs of people by providing a physically safe working environment, by providing security of income, and by making people feel welcome and appreciated while they are at work.

4. *Self-Esteem.* Self-esteem refers to the need to feel valuable, important, appreciated, and approved of. It is called a "being need" by Maslow. It is only when a person moves to satisfy self-esteem needs for doing a good job, for excelling, for standing out on the basis of individual performance and contribution that a person begins to grow.

The very best definition of self-esteem is "how much you like yourself." The more you like and respect yourself, the higher your self-esteem. The higher your self-esteem, the better you do your work. The more you like yourself, the more you like others. The more you like yourself and others, the more they like you right back and want to work with you and for you. The roots of self-esteem are discussed in depth in Chapter 4.

5. *Self-Actualization.* Initially, the *highest* level of need that Maslow identified in his hierarchy was self-actualization. Self-actualization can be defined as a feeling that "you are becoming all that you are capable of becoming."

There is within each person an innate drive to fulfill his full potential as an individual. It is only when a person feels that he is living at the very highest and best level that he possibly can that he feels truly happy, inspired, and motivated.

When a person is learning, growing, stretching, and achieving more than she has in the past, she feels that she is working at the outer edge of her potential. She has a feeling of self-actualization.

Self-actualized people tend to be happy, calm, positive, creative, objective about themselves, clear-eyed, honest, and genuinely respectful and appreciative of other people. According to Maslow, self-actualization is the highest level of need that we can attain, and it is something we strive toward throughout our lives.

Self-actualization needs are the one set of needs that can never be fully satisfied. Even when a person feels that he is fulfilling his potential, he keeps setting bigger and more challenging goals; he wants to do, be, and have something more. And every step he takes toward greater self-actualization, the happier and more motivated he is to do even more.

The Major Motivator

America today is a magnet for talented people from 174 countries who flock to these shores, both legally and illegally, so that they can have an opportunity to enjoy the "American dream."

It is commonly believed that the primary motivation for uprooting oneself and moving to the United States is money. But at least since the 1950s, when people were asked why they moved to the United States, the most common reason cited was because "in the United States, your potential is unlimited."

A major reason that people go to work with a company, and stay with that company a long time, is because the company continuously opens up opportunities for them that make them feel that within that company, their potential is unlimited as well.

Frustrated Expectations

Conversely, many psychologists agree that a primary source of negative emotions is a feeling of frustrated expectations.

For example, a person takes a job with the expectation that in this job she would be able to fulfill her full potential. She would be able to learn and grow and earn more money. But for various reasons, it did not work out. The job turned out to be boring and repetitive. There was no chance for advancement. When a person feels that she has far more to contribute than the company gives in return, in terms of the opportunity to contribute, the individual becomes frustrated, angry, and counterproductive. And the more talent the person has, the more frustrated she becomes.

Maslow's hierarchy of needs explains why and how people are motivated to behave the way they do. It gives ideas and guidelines you can use to create a better work environment and to structure jobs in such a way that the higher needs of each person are being fulfilled. Everything in this book is aimed at giving you the tools you need to create a peak performance workplace, based on these discoveries.

Theory X and Theory Y

In the 1960s, Frederick Herzberg, an organizational psychologist, came up with a definition of motivational psychology that also still influences us today. He said that there were two views of human motivation: Theory X and Theory Y. Whichever of these views you held would largely determine the way you treated other people.

Theory X, which is based on thousands of years of human history, right up through the Industrial Revolution, said that individual workers were lazy, untrustworthy, and undependable. They had to be carefully organized, managed, and supervised. They had to work within the constraints of very clear rewards and punishments.

Under Theory X, workers were considered to be unreliable and in need of constant supervision. They were provided with minimum working conditions, paid the very least possible, and quickly replaced if they proved to be uncooperative or unproductive. There are still many managers who have this view of human nature. It is the typical carrot-and-stick view of treating people.

Herzberg's great contribution was the idea of the Theory Y person. Under Theory Y, individuals were seen to be honest, hardworking, well-meaning, productive, and desirous of doing a good job for the company. All they required was that the company provided them with a safe, secure, comfortable work environment within which they could perform at their best.

Hygiene Factors

Herzberg also identified the concept of "hygiene factors." During his time, many employers thought that providing a clean and safe work environment, a steady paycheck, and a good job was sufficient motivation. Herzberg dismissed these as hygiene factors, basic requirements to guard against *demotivation,* but having very little motivational capability at all. To motivate people, according to Herzberg, you had to appeal to their "motivation needs." Motivation needs included interesting, challenging work, enjoyable and friendly coworkers, opportunity for growth and advancement, and a high-respect, high-trust workplace.

Whereas people would come to work and do their jobs if you provided them with the basic hygiene factors, satisfying the deficiency needs identified in Maslow's hierarchy, they would only perform at their best and do a terrific job when you made the work fun, enjoyable, challenging, and interesting—in other words, when you satisfied their growth needs as well as their hygiene needs.

Does Money Make the Mare Go?

Many managers have felt, for many years, that money is the major motivator of production and performance at work. They think: "Just give people enough money and they will produce at a high level."

To test the validity of this idea, consider this story. In one company, on a Monday morning, everyone in the factory was called together before they started work. The manager stood up and announced that, effective immediately, to encourage workers to be more productive, the company was doubling the salaries of everyone in the plant.

Did doubling the salaries increase productivity? Yes, it did, but only for *one hour*. Within one hour of the pay raise, productivity levels went back to where they had been before, and never increased again. Giving people additional money, all by itself, does not have a long-lasting impact on productivity and performance.

Theory Z

Theory X says that people are lazy and undependable, and that they must be continually supervised and monitored if you want them to do their jobs properly. Theory Y says that people are good, hardworking, and desirous of making a valuable contribution if you just treat them properly.

In my estimation, the truth is closer to "Theory Z." This is my own contribution to management motivation, and it is based on what I call the *expediency factor*. That is, individuals are expedient; they will always take the fastest and easiest way to get the things that they want right now, with little concern for the long-term consequences of their behaviors.

What this means is that, basically, people are very much the same in terms of motivation. Everyone wants to enjoy safety, security, belongingness, self-esteem, and self-actualization. Everyone wants to be successful, happy, and respected in their work. And people will do *whatever* they feel they need to do to achieve those goals. Your job as the manager is to provide the environment where individuals are *internally* motivated to do the very best job possible, in the very best spirit possible, to make the very best contribution possible.

Internal versus External Motivation

Today, more than ever before, people are motivated *internally* to do the very best job possible. The old external motivators of job security and "carrot-and-stick management" only apply to new workers doing basic jobs that require little skill or mental involvement.

In your workplace today, the people around you do their jobs because they want to, not because they have to. They do their jobs well because they feel internally challenged and externally appreciated. People respect their jobs and treat their companies well because you respect them and you treat them well. What is there about this idea that is hard to understand?

Your job is to create a work environment where the negative factors that detract from performance are taken away, the neutral factors that are the minimum essentials of a job are satisfied, and the motivators are maximized.

In this environment, people will be internally motivated and stimulated to make the most valuable contribution to your company that they possibly can.

Action Exercises

1. Identify your happiest and most productive employee. What are the factors in this person's work environment that contribute to this high level of performance?

2. Identify the things you do to satisfy the financial and emotional security needs of your team members.

3. Identify the actions you can take to increase the feeling of belongingness of the members of your team.

4. Decide on one thing you are going to do each day to raise the self-esteem of one or more of your team members.

5. Identify specific actions you can take to make people's jobs more challenging and interesting.

6. Identify the parts of your job that you do well and enjoy the most. How could you organize your time so that you could do more of these things, more of the time?

7. At your next staff meeting, ask everyone around the table this "president for a day" question: "If you were president for a day, what one thing would you change about your job or the business?" Be prepared for some eye-opening answers.

CHAPTER THREE

Ignite the Flame of Personal Performance

"Pretend that every person you meet has a sign around his or
her neck that says, 'Make me feel important.' Not only will
you succeed in sales; you will succeed in life."

—MARY KAY ASH

Your job as a manager is to get the very highest quality and
quantity of performance and output from the human resources entrusted to you. As much as 80 percent of the operating costs of your business are represented by the wages,
salaries, benefits, and bonuses paid out to your people. Small,
incremental increases in individual performance can have a
substantial effect on your bottom line.

To get the very most out of others, you must develop a

solid understanding of how you became the person you are today and, by extension, how others have become the people they are as well. You have to develop a fairly good idea of how people think, feel, and react. You need to know why people do, or don't do, things and how you can influence them in a positive way.

People Are Like Icebergs

It's not easy. Individuals are incredibly complex. They have been formed and shaped mentally and emotionally by thousands of small and large experiences. Every thought, feeling, emotion, success, failure, fear, desire, and experience going back to childhood has had an influence on how the person in front of you became the way he is today. This is equally true for you, too.

Imagine that each person who reports to you is like an iceberg. Only 10 percent of the iceberg is visible above the surface. The other 90 percent, which you cannot see, understand, or influence, is under the water, in the past experiences and subconscious of the person in front of you.

Never try to be a psychologist to your staff. You should understand in general how your employees think and why they act the way they do, but you are not qualified to give them advice and counsel, or to try to help them become something that they are not. Besides, it doesn't do any good. People are the way they are as the result of a thousand influences over which you have no control.

People Don't Change

The basic rule is: "People don't change." As comedian Flip Wilson said, "What you sees is what you gets."

Many of the problems between people in work, marriage,

and relationships could be quickly solved if either or both of the parties involved were to accept this simple fact.

If a person is lazy, he will always be lazy. If a person is late, she will always be late. If a person is dishonest, the person will always be dishonest. If people are messy or do a poor job, they will always be messy and always do a poor job. People don't change.

Under stress, people not only do not change, they become even *more* of what they already are. If they are already rigid, they become even more rigid when things don't work out the way they want. If they are weak or irresolute, they become weaker and even more irresolute in the face of adversity and setbacks.

There is an old saying out on the farm: "Never try to teach a pig to fly, for two reasons. First, it doesn't do any good. The pig is never going to fly. And second, it just irritates the pig."

Even if people offer to change, promise to change, agree to change, and try to change, they don't change. They remain the way they are. It has taken most people an entire lifetime to become who they are today, and they are not going to change, no matter how you try to impact or influence them.

The Purpose of Learning and Developing

Sometimes, people confront me and argue with me against this rule. They say, "If people don't change, what is the purpose of education, motivation, team building, and all the other things that we do to get people to perform better or differently?"

The explanation is simple. By about the age of sixteen or seventeen, the basic personality of a person is fixed like concrete. People's temperament and personality style remain constant for the rest of their lives, in most cases. If you ever go to a high school reunion after twenty or thirty years, you will be constantly amused to notice that the people you went to high school with have not changed at all, except physically. They still have the same ways of talking, laughing, listening, joking, and relating to others. They are still the same.

What you can influence are their natural talents, skills, and abilities. You can teach people and encourage them to be even better than they have been in the past by helping them to develop along their own natural lines of talent and ability. But you cannot turn a basketball player into a musician or an angry person into a friendly person. These are largely fixed characteristics that do not alter in the course of time.

Large companies often hire people based on their personality, temperament, and basic abilities, and then invest many years in training and developing them into becoming valuable members of the corporate team. They don't try to turn ducks into eagles. They hire eagles and then teach them to fly in formation.

How do people become the way they are? What are the essential determinants of human performance and behavior? Your ability to understand the foundation principles of human behavior can give you an edge in selecting people and molding them into a peak performance team for yourself and your business.

The Master Program of Success

The discovery of the "self-concept" was one of the most important breakthroughs in psychology in the twentieth century. It turns out that each person has a self-concept that largely precedes and predicts that person's performance in every area. All changes and improvements in performance begin with changes and improvements in the self-concept of the individual.

The self-concept is made up of all of the thoughts, feelings, desires, actions, experiences, and decisions made by the individual, starting in infancy and often before. There is evidence to suggest that infants in the womb know if they are wanted and awaited even before they are born. The child born into a world where both parents are eager to have that child develops a more positive and more confident personality than a child who feels unwanted for any reason.

The self-concept is the key to understanding human personality, performance, productivity, and happiness. Each person behaves on the outside exactly as he thinks about himself on the inside. Each person looks at the world through a latticework or prism of all past experiences, especially the experience of the moment. A person's previous experiences may have been right or wrong, good or bad, true or false, but to the degree to which the individual *believes* that something is true for him, he acts consistent with that belief.

For you to release more of the potential of each person who reports to you, you must understand how the self-concept of the person works, and how you can influence it in a positive way. The self-concept, the bundle of beliefs that serves as the master program of the mental computer of the individual, is made up of three parts: the self-ideal, the self-image, and the self-esteem. Let's examine each of them in turn.

The Self-Ideal

Each person has within her an *ideal* of the very best person she could possibly be. This ideal can be defined as "the person you would like most to become." Successful, happy people are very clear about their ideals. They know exactly what they believe in and stand for, and what they will not stand for. As a result of this level of clarity, they are more confident and more positive than the average person. Top people, leaders, have very clear self-ideals.

The self-ideal is made up of all the virtues, values, principles, and qualities that the individual considers to be important and valuable to himself and others. In addition, the self-ideal is made up of the goals, dreams, hopes, aspirations, and thoughts about the possible future of the individual.

When a person is clear about her self-ideal, she strives toward becoming more and more like that ideal, both consciously and unconsciously. She admires other people who manifest and demonstrate the qualities that she most aspires to herself. She is attracted to people who have the same values that she does. She is inspired by people who demonstrate those values in their behaviors.

The Importance of the Role Model

The most successful people in any society tend to most admire and respect other people, living or dead, who have lived admirable lives and who became highly respected people as a result of their character and accomplishments. Aristotle said, "All improvement in society begins with the improvement of the character of the young." And the young are greatly influenced by the role models in their lives during their formative years.

This is why one of the most important parts of the self-ideal is the role model. Human beings naturally admire and look up to men and women who represent the most important qualities to which they aspire, and who demonstrate these qualities in their behavior.

One of the most important jobs of the manager is to *set an example* for the way people are supposed to act in an organization. The manager must set an example for the way people are to be treated and the way the job is to be done. When the manager sets high standards of integrity, honesty, and quality, and encourages all people on the team to aspire to those qualities for themselves and their work, he creates a positive workplace that's very different from the one where values, virtues, and principles are largely ignored and not talked about.

Building Companies That Inspire the Self-Ideal

To satisfy this natural human drive for ideals to aspire toward, the best companies develop clear values, vision, mission, purpose, and goals.

Defining Clear Values. In their book *The Power of Ethical Management,* Ken Blanchard and Norman Vincent Peale examined the profitability of hundreds of companies, comparing them to other companies in the same industries. They found that the companies that had clear values, written as policy, with definitions of how those values were to be practiced in day-to-day business, were consistently more profitable over the decades than those companies that *may* have had similar values, but whose values were not written down, discussed, or understood by the people who worked there.

Some years ago, I worked with a company that started with an idea, raised money from interested investors, and went on to become and remain one of the most successful companies in the communications industry in America. I learned that before they formed their company, the key people sat down and agreed on the five values that they would use to guide their behavior and decision making in the months and years ahead. After many hours of discussion and negotiation, the five values were selected and then organized by priority. They then took it one step further. They developed a one-line statement explaining how that value would be practiced in daily operations and activities.

They then printed the values and their definitions on laminated cards that were handed out to every person in the company. Whenever two people in the company had to make a decision, they would take out their laminated value cards and review the decision against the five values. They would even go through this process on the phone. Only after they had compared the decision they were considering against each value would they make a final determination.

Not unsurprisingly, the people in this company, at all levels, were some of the happiest, most positive, most productive people I had ever worked with. And in addition, they were consistently profitable, year after year, in very competitive markets.

You only need three to five values around which you build your organization. The determination of these values may take several hours of discussion and debate and may be undertaken during strategic planning meetings with large corporations. But in every case, at the end of the discussion, the entire executive group must be unanimous in their choice of values, and their order of priority.

Developing a Clear Vision. The second step in creating an ideal of your company toward which employees can aspire is for you to create a *vision* of what your company will look like sometime in the future, based on your values.

The best leaders practice *idealization*. They project forward five or more years into the future and imagine that their business is perfect in every way. They imagine that they could wave a magic wand and five years from today the company would have the best products, best people, best leaders, best customer service, best systems, best reputation, best levels of profitability, and the best stock price. They then come back to the present and ask the question of substance: WWH2H, or What Would Have to Happen?

You cannot create an ideal company unless you have a clear picture of what that company will look like when it is ideal in every way. The ideal product or service offering becomes a core part of this long-term vision, since fully 90 percent of the success of any business is determined by having a great product or service in the first place.

Finding Your Mission. Based on the values and vision of your company, you can then identify an inspiring core mission for the company. A mission must have a clear, achievable goal that everyone can aim at accomplishing. A mission must also have a *measure* so that you can determine how close you are to accomplishing the mission.

When AT&T began expanding telephone service throughout the United States more than 100 years ago, its mission was "to bring a telephone within the reach of every American." When it finally achieved this goal by the 1960s, it failed to replace the old mission with a new mission. As a result, the company began to drift and to focus more on politics and profits than on serving people. Very soon, new competitors entered the market to contest the AT&T monopoly, which was no longer justifiable. In a few years, the company was broken up and replaced by small and large telephone companies all over the country.

Finding a Purpose That Inspires You. What is your purpose for being in business in the first place? The purpose of your business flows out of the values, vision, and mission that you have defined as the ideal for your future organization. Your purpose is the answer to the question, *Why* are we doing this at all? Your mission clearly defines what it is you and your organization are trying to accomplish, and your purpose determines why you are trying to accomplish it.

Your purpose should affect you, and your people, *emotionally*. It should keep you up at night. You should want to do more and more of it, and become better and better at it. Your greatest satisfaction or joy in your business life comes from fulfilling your purpose and by hearing other people tell you that you did.

Over the years, people have asked me for my reason or purpose for being in business. My answer hasn't changed in more than twenty-five years: "My purpose is to help people achieve their goals *faster* than they ever would have in the absence of my help."

This purpose statement may sound a little bit awkward, but it has informed, inspired, and guided every seminar, audio, video, and written piece of material that I have produced in thirty years. It has been the driving force behind every talk and training session that I have given, in fifty-five countries to more than five million people.

Determining Your Goals. Your goals are the specific time-bounded, measurable *objectives* that you need to accomplish to demonstrate your values, realize the vision, fulfill the mission, and achieve the purpose. Your goals are the focal points of your day-to-day activities in every area of your business. Your ability to set and achieve your most important goals is strongly influenced by the degree of clarity you have with regard to why you are striving for those goals in the first place.

Employees with a Self-Ideal

The best people in any company are those who are completely committed to the values, vision, mission, purpose, and goals of the organization. They come to work each day excited to participate in helping the company achieve those goals in some way. Their greatest satisfaction is in knowing that they are making an important contribution toward making the company a great company, especially in terms of how it is defined by your customers and the people who use your products and services.

A clear, exciting, inspiring, uplifting vision, combined with a mission, purpose, and goals, is the key to satisfying one of the deepest subconscious needs that people have, which is to aspire toward and to achieve high ideals in every part of their work and personal life.

Your Self-Image Determines Your Performance

The self-image is the second part of the self-concept. It exerts an inordinate influence on the thoughts, feelings and behaviors of each person. Your self-image is defined as "how you see yourself" prior to any situation of importance and whenever you are actively engaged in a particular behavior.

Your self-image is often called your "inner mirror." This is the mirror that you look into subconsciously to determine how you should behave in a given situation. Just as actors and actresses take a last quick look at themselves in a large mirror before they go onto the stage, we too take a glance at our inner mirrors to tell us how to behave in whatever it is we are about to do.

In his breakthrough work and book on *The Magic Power of Self-Image Psychology,* Dr. Maxwell Maltz demonstrated that people always act on the outside based on the way they see themselves on the *inside,* even if the way they see themselves is inaccurate.

Maltz's discovery came about as a result of his work as a plastic surgeon. He would often operate on people with facial problems that made them appear unattractive. Surgery transformed these men and women so that they looked handsome or beautiful. But then he was surprised to find that his patients were just as negative and unhappy about their appearance as they had been before the operation. What was going on?

What he found was that if people did not change the way they saw themselves on the inside, nothing changed for them on the *outside*. If they saw themselves as unattractive on the inside, they would expect other people to see them as unattractive and undesirable on the outside. It was only when they changed their thinking about themselves on the inside that they began to experience newer and happier experiences on the outside.

The Way Your Parents Looked at You

Your self-image is formed from early childhood, from the first time you look into the face of your parents and see them looking back at you. When parents respond to their children in a happy, laughing, and delighted way, treating their children as though they are beautiful, intelligent, wonderful human beings, the child's self-image begins to form in a very healthy way. He sees himself as positive, attractive, intelligent, and desirable. This becomes his worldview. As a result, the child interacts with other people as though he is already popular and well liked.

Throughout your childhood, you are strongly influenced by people you respect and whose opinions you value. You start with your parents. If your parents treat you as though you are valuable and important, and continually praise and compliment you, you grow up with a positive self-image that carries over into your interactions with others.

If there are people in your childhood—siblings, unhappy

relatives, or members of your peer group—who treat you in a negative, rude, or unpleasant way, it can shake your self-image and self-confidence at an early age and cause you to question yourself. Fortunately, the stronger and more positive your self-image is as a result of your childhood conditioning, the greater resistance you have to the negative behaviors of others. You maintain a strong, positive self-image even if people are negative toward you for any reason.

The Three Parts of the Self-Image

The first part of self-image is the way you see *yourself*. This perception is most important, and it may or may not be based on reality. You may see yourself in a positive and realistic way, as self-actualizing people do, or you may see yourself in a negative and pessimistic way, as unhappy people do.

My father grew up in a difficult home. He had a negative self-image all his life, and he passed it on to his children, as most parents do. For years, he would tell me that I was unreliable, undependable, a liar, and a thief. It didn't matter that the incidences were as small as having not remembered something accurately, or taking a cookie from the cookie jar. As far as my father was concerned, I was no good. As a result, I grew up with a negative self-image and with feelings of inadequacy and inferiority in comparison with other kids who came from better homes.

In my early teens, I had a great revelation. I realized that nothing that my father said to me, about me, was necessarily true. I did not have to be influenced by his negativity and his disparaging comments. I developed a mental Teflon shield. I decided to ignore and throw off his negative comments and instead replace them with positive pictures of myself doing well in the things that I tried. This decision changed my life, as it changes the life of every person who tries it.

Writing Your Own Script. Remember, almost nothing negative that people say about you (or said about you when you were young) is true or permanently true. At any time, you can decide to rewrite the script of your own life. As psychologist and philosopher William James of Harvard University once said, "In the past I was this, but from now on I will be that."

Were you late for appointments in the past? Well, now you will be punctual for every appointment. Were you messy and disorganized when you were growing up? Well, now you will be neat and well organized. Did you have a tendency to hold back when other people were speaking, guarding your opinion? Well, now you can speak positively and confidently and express yourself freely and clearly.

Here is the great news. Anything you do repeatedly, over and over, eventually becomes a new habit. As long as you have the seed of the desire to improve your performance on the outside, you can grow that seed on the inside by repetition and practice. Eventually, your new desired visualized behavior takes hold and becomes a permanent part of your personality and your character. You can actually shape or sculpt yourself into the kind of person you want to be by repeatedly "seeing yourself" as that person. You can change your outer performance by changing your inner picture.

How Others See You. The second part of the self-image is how you *think* other people see you.

This, too, is very important. If you think that other people see you in a positive way, you will tend to act in a positive way. If you think that people like you, respect you, and look up to you, you will tend to be a positive, pleasant, personable individual in every interaction.

Because we are so strongly influenced by the behaviors and opinions of other people toward us when we are growing up,

as adults we are unduly influenced by how we think other people are thinking about us. Many people are so sensitive to the
thoughts and opinions of other people that they cannot take
any kind of independent action without being assured of approval in advance.

Deciding for Yourself. The fact is that you should never do or
not do anything because you are afraid of what other people
might think about you. When you are in your twenties, you are
very sensitive to how people might think about you. When you
are in your thirties, you are less sensitive to the opinions of
others and care less about how other people think about you.
But when you get into your forties, you learn the great truth:
Nobody was really thinking about you at all.

The fact is that people spend 99 percent of their time thinking about *themselves* and their own personal concerns. They
divide up the other one percent of the attention that they have
among the rest of humanity, including you. One of the greatest
of all vanities is for a person to think that other people spend
a lot of time thinking about them. The fact is that most people
are so busy with their own lives that they have no time to think
about you at all.

How People Really See You. The third part of your self-image
is the way that people *really* do see you. You may think yourself
to be an average performer at your company, and then be surprised to find that the people around you consider you to be a
top performer in what you do. On the other hand, you may
feel that you are doing a good job and then find, to your surprise, that the people around you consider you to be a below-
average part of the team.

The ideal for a balanced personality is when the way you
see *yourself,* the way you think *others* see you, and the way
others *actually* do see you are all in harmony. When this oc-

curs, the way you think and feel about yourself will be exactly the way others think and feel about you and treat you on a day-to-day basis.

Self-Image and Self-Ideal in Harmony

Here is a great discovery. There is a direct relationship between how good you feel about yourself and how closely your self-image is consistent with your self-ideal.

Each time that you do something that is *more* consistent with the person you would ideally like to be in the future, your self-image improves. You feel better about yourself. You feel happier and more confident. You are more motivated and inspired to engage in those same behaviors that are even more consistent with the very best person you could possibly be.

When the manager tells a person that she did a great job in a particular area, which is the self-ideal of most people, the individual's self-image improves. The individual feels validated and appreciated. The individual feels happier and more confident, and more eager to do an even better job in the future.

The way the manager treats staff members has an inordinate effect on their overall self-image as well. When we are children, we look into the faces and listen to the voices of our parents to find out if we are good, desirable, intelligent, or safe in our world.

When we become adults, we transfer this expectation to the workplace and our boss becomes our new "parent." We then look into the face and listen to the voice of the boss to find out how good we are and how well we are doing. For this reason, the boss can strongly influence the self-image, and thereby the performance, of the team member. The more the boss treats the team member as if he was an excellent person, the more the person's self-image is reinforced, and the more positive and productive the team member become.

Your Self-Esteem Is the Core

The reactor core of the personality is the self-esteem, the feelings or emotions of the individual. It is the emotions that determine the personality of the individual. A person with high self-esteem is a positive, high-energy, creative, and productive person in the workplace. A person with low self-esteem has feelings of inferiority and inadequacy, lacks self-confidence, and feels insecure and unsafe.

The best definition of self-esteem is "how much you like yourself." The more you like yourself, the more you like other people. The more you like other people, the more they like you right back. The more you like other people, the better a team player you will be. The more you like yourself, the better and more valuable results you achieve at work.

The biggest single obstacle to the full development of the personality of the individual is that feeling of not liking oneself very much. Because of childhood experiences, especially the way the child was treated by his parents, children often grow up with deep-down feelings of inferiority. The next chapter covers in detail how the formative years impact the self-esteem of a person—and how we can take lessons from what we know of how self-esteem is built in the young and apply them to the workplace.

Self-Esteem and Self-Efficacy

There is a direct relationship between self-esteem and *self-efficacy*. The more you like yourself in your work, the better you do your job. And the better you do your job, the more you like yourself. Each time you learn and practice something new that enables you to do your job even better, not only does your self-efficacy improve, but your self-esteem goes up at the same time.

Each person has a deep-down need to feel effective; people want to feel that they are competent and capable of doing their work and achieving their goals. We strive for this feeling of self-efficacy all of our lives. It is only when we really believe that we are good at what we do that we feel confident and happy about ourselves.

There is a direct relationship between the way you see yourself, your *self-image,* and the person you would like most to become (the way you would like to see yourself) sometime in the future, your *self-ideal.* The more you feel that your behaviors, day in and day out, are more consistent with your becoming the very best person you could possibly be, the more you begin to like yourself, and value and esteem yourself, and the more positive your personality becomes in every area. Because of this interrelationship of the different parts of the personality, perhaps the most important job of the manager in building a top team is to continually reinforce the self-esteem, self-image, and self-ideal of each person on the team.

Creating a Peak Performance Workplace

To create a peak performance person, team, and work environment, three things are necessary:

1. Each person must be clear and committed to the values, vision, mission, purpose, and goals of the company. Developing this clarity is a primary responsibility of management.

2. You as the manager must continually reinforce a positive self-image in each person on the team. You must make your team members see themselves as valuable, worthy, and com-

petent, and getting better and better every day and every week.

3. You must continually build, support, and reinforce the self-esteem of each person so that your team members like themselves even more as the result of the way you treat them in every interaction.

Everything counts. As the manager, everything you do or say either builds people up or pulls them down. Concerning your behaviors and the emotions of the people who report to you, nothing is *neutral*. Every interaction is emotionally charged in some way. Because you have power over the other person, everything that you say of a positive or negative nature will have an immediate and often long-term positive or negative effect on the other person.

Remember, there are only four ways to change any situation. You can do *more of* something from which you are getting good results. You can do *less of* something else from which you are not getting good results. You can *start* doing something that you are not doing today. Or you can *stop* doing something else altogether that is no longer helpful. In every workforce, every manager should ask himself those four questions, every single day: What should I be doing: More of? Less of? What should I start doing? What should I stop doing altogether?

Your job as a manager is to recognize that self-concept is the master program of a person's subconscious computer. Everything you do or say has an effect in stimulating or shaping that self-concept. Your words and behavior either improve performance or they lower performance. When you are continuously aware of how your thoughts, words, and behaviors affect the feelings and behaviors of others, you become a better manager who helps people perform at their best over and over again.

Action Exercises

1. Select one behavior that you feel interferes with how effective you could be as manager and resolve to stop it completely.

2. Identify the three most important managerial qualities that you would like to have or acquire. What could you do each day to develop these qualities?

3. Create a clear, exciting vision for the future of your company, and determine the purpose, the "why," of your business.

4. Treat each person with an attitude of positive expectations. Tell your staff members how good they are and what a great job they do.

5. Build self-esteem in the members of your team by treating them as if they were extremely valuable to the success of the business.

6. Act as if you were a loving parent to your staff; treat them as if they were good children and you really appreciate them.

7. Reinforce their self-images by continually pointing out their successes, what they are doing well, and what a difference they make to your business.

CHAPTER FOUR

Make People Feel Important

"Those who are not looking for happiness are the most likely
to find it, because those who are searching forget that the
surest way to be happy is to seek happiness for others."

—MARTIN LUTHER KING JR.

The key to keep motivating people to perform at their best
is to build self-esteem (which leads to self-confidence and
self-respect) in each person who reports to you. Each person
has unlimited potential that the individual can bring to bear
on the job to do that job better and faster. People have huge
reservoirs of creativity that can be unleashed to solve problems, overcome obstacles, and achieve business goals.

Knowledge workers on your team are motivated more internally than they are externally. They perform at their best
because they *want* to perform at their best. The fact is that

you cannot motivate people; you can only create the environment where motivation takes place naturally and spontaneously.

The Leader Sets the Tone

The leader is the most important person in any organization. The leader sets the tone by the way he talks, behaves, responds to others, and treats people every day. People tend to "follow the leader" in that they imitate or mimic the behavior of the leader toward others. When the leader treats other people with courtesy and respect, everyone eventually begins treating coworkers with the same courtesy and respect.

There are specific behaviors that leaders can practice each day, and in each interaction, to make people feel good about themselves. When you deliberately take the time and make the effort to build self-esteem in other people and simultaneously eliminate the fears that hold people back from putting their whole hearts into their work, a peak performance work environment blooms naturally around you, like flowers in the spring.

Remember, there are only *four* ways to change or improve any situation. You can do more of some things. You can do less of other things. You can start doing something brand-new, something that you have never done before. Or, you can stop doing certain things altogether.

You can begin the process of building people's self-esteem by *not* doing certain things. The three things that you should never do at work are to criticize, complain about, or condemn the personal behavior of another person.

Destructive Criticism Hurts

The military has a nuclear weapon called a neutron bomb. This bomb can be detonated over a populated area with great power and impact. The difference between the neutron bomb and other atomic bombs is that the neutron bomb kills all the people, but leaves the buildings intact.

Jack Welch, the past CEO of General Electric, was often called "Neutron Jack" because, in the massive restructuring of the business, he shut down entire underperforming divisions, laying off all the people, but leaving the buildings intact.

Destructive criticism is like a neutron bomb as well. The worst behavior that a person can experience, the true destroyer of personality and character, is *destructive criticism.* Destructive criticism is the root cause of most feelings of low self-esteem, poor self-image, inferiority, inadequacy, incompetence, and unhappiness in life. Only in this sense, it leaves the victim standing up and walking around, but destroys the personality inside.

Problems in Adult Life

Virtually all problems in adult life can be traced back to destructive criticism in early childhood. When the child is told over and over by one or both parents that he is bad, no good, undependable, unreliable, and dishonest, or any other negative description, the child is unable to defend himself emotionally against these attacks. The child is too small and vulnerable, and too receptive to the messages sent to him continually by his parents. His little mind accepts and absorbs these criticisms as irrefutable truths. They become part of the child's self-concept, accepted without question, and often form a permanent part of his self-image and worldview. Whenever you see an uncertain, insecure, negative, or fearful adult, you can immediately assume that person was once a child who was continually attacked and emotionally beaten down with criticism by his parents.

Many parents have no idea how destructive their words can be. Most parents want their children to grow up happy, positive, confident, and capable of being successful as adults. They have no idea that the continuous, ongoing criticism that becomes a part of their daily interaction with their children is eroding away the self-esteem and self-confidence that makes success in adult life possible.

Why Children Lie

When my wife, Barbara, and I had young children, we found out that children do not always tell their parents the whole truth, or any of the truth at all. They tell stories, half-truths, and complete falsehoods. Every parent has had this experience. It seems to go along with child raising. When it happens, you start questioning your child-raising skills.

Then we came across a magazine article on parenting. It asked, "If your children lie to you, *who* has made them afraid to tell the truth?"

Both Barbara and I had been raised in families with parents who were highly critical and negative, who complained about and criticized our behaviors all the time we were growing up. When we read that question, we realized that "the sins of the fathers were being passed on to the children." We had slipped into the habit of criticizing and berating our children when they did something that we thought was wrong or disagreed with. At that moment we decided that we would break the vicious cycle of criticism that triggered anger, defensiveness, and lying, and abolish it from our household.

We immediately sat down with our two young children and told them that we would never criticize them again. We told them that they would never get into trouble for telling the truth. We told them that as long as they told the truth, we would always support them and approve of them.

Children Will Try You Out

Children being children, they were a bit skeptical of our promises. So they tried us out with an occasional *small* truth. If they got into trouble at school or broke something, they would come and tell us and watch carefully to see how we reacted. We kept our word. We never criticized them again for making a mistake of any kind. We thanked them and praised them for telling the truth. Within a couple of months, our children began telling us the truth about almost everything that was going on in their lives. Telling the truth became part of their personalities. They soon became known as the most honest and truthful kids in their social circles.

As adults, our children have developed wonderful reputations for honesty and integrity among everyone who knows them. They always say calmly and clearly what they are thinking. They will talk with the same straightforwardness to ex-U.S. presidents as they do to casual visitors. They have no fear at all of meeting and interacting with strangers, no matter what their stature or position. By refusing to criticize them for anything, we have been able to drive out the fear that often sabotages the thoughts, feelings, and behaviors of young people.

This advice applies equally to your *staff.* If they do not tell you the complete truth, who has made them afraid to speak out? Resolve today, and set it as a policy in your company, that no one will ever be punished in any way for telling the truth. Encourage staff members to be open and honest at all times, especially with bad news.

Destruction in Many Forms

Destructive criticism comes in many forms. It may be specific and direct, where the child is told that she is no good or bad in some way. It may be implied by an attitude, disapproval, disrespect, or criticism of the child's person, dress, or behavior. It is quite common that the child, even as an adult, continually rehashes and revisits the stream of continuous criticism she received earlier, reliving the criticism and keeping it alive right into adulthood. This feeling is summarized in perhaps the worst self-concept that a person can develop, "I'm not good enough."

This feeling of "I'm not good enough" is the root of feelings of inadequacy, inferiority, negativity, shyness, unattractiveness, and unpopularity. It is the reason that, no matter how successful some people are, they can never stop wanting more and more. They try in everything they do to silence that voice that says, "I'm not good enough."

Destructive criticism may be *imagined,* in that the individual anticipates being criticized for something that could fail and cause him not to like himself. He therefore avoids engaging in that behavior at all. Criticism may be anticipated because the individual fears that if he does or does not do something, someone in his life will be displeased and express disapproval of him.

Destructive criticism is the fertile soil in which grow all of the negative emotions. Destructive criticism promotes and multiplies the fears of failure and rejection. The thought or experience of destructive criticism makes a person feel angry and defensive, sometimes for years and even decades. Destructive criticism leads to feelings of inferiority that trigger the negative emotions of envy and resentment, especially of others who seem to be more successful. Destructive criticism and the feelings of inferiority that it triggers lead to jealousy of others who seem to be doing better than the individual experiencing this negative emotion.

Criticism Travels Fast

Time is measured in increments. An hour is reduced to the minute to the second to the millisecond to the nanosecond. But the shortest increment of time is the amount of time it takes for a rumor to spread in an organization. Anything done or said in the head office that can affect the life or work of someone, even on the other side of the country, will be relayed to that person with the speed of summer lightning, before you could pick up the phone and call the person directly.

At work, criticism of another person also spreads with the same speed. Anything that you say that is negative about anyone, anywhere, anytime, even over dinner in a small secluded restaurant, will get back to that person faster than you can imagine. You must be careful about leveling any form of criticism, complaint, or condemnation of other people if you expect to get the best out of them.

Looking for the Good

As a manager, the first step you can take to get the best out of others is to eliminate destructive criticism from your vocabulary, for any reason. Resolve today that you will never criticize, attack, insult, or diminish another person for any reason. Instead, you will look for something good in everything that happens.

You have heard that the optimist sees the glass as half-full, and the pessimist sees the glass as half-empty. What is equally important is that the best managers think about problems as things to be solved and difficulties to be overcome. The worst managers approach problems in terms of what happened and *who is to blame.* The very act of focusing your thinking and conversation away from the problem and onto the solution transforms you from a pessimist to an optimist in a few seconds.

If you were to make one decision about your behavior that would, more than anything else, have a greater impact on your relationships, both at home and at work, it would be to immediately decide that from now on, you will never criticize anyone for anything. When you slip up, as you will from time to time, immediately go and take back what you said. Go to the other person and say, "I apologize for what I said. I should not have spoken to you in that way. I have no excuses. Please accept my apology."

This simple response by you, which requires tremendous ego strength, immediately neutralizes the situation and puts it back onto an even keel.

No More Complaining

The second thing that you stop doing is complaining for any reason. In working with thousands of people in seminars and workshops over the years, I have found that people who complain a lot today were probably raised by a parent who complained a lot when they were growing up. Because children imitate the dominant parent, they come to conclude that complaining is the natural response when you are unhappy or displeased with anything. From then on, they complain continually about both large and small things.

They get into the habit of playing "ain't it awful." In this game, each person in the conversation complains about something in life. Then the next person complains about something even worse. This goes around and around, with each person trying to top the other with a complaint about their health, finances, jobs, and, mostly, other people.

Birds of a Feather

Complainers are always looking for something or someone to complain about. They tend to associate with other complainers. They talk together at work and socialize after work. They go out for lunch and coffee breaks together. Complaining becomes the basis of their relationships and conversation.

But there is a major problem with both criticizing and complaining. In both situations, when you do it, you are positioning yourself as a *victim*. When you complain, you are saying, "Ain't it awful; I am a victim of this situation. Look what has happened to me."

When you complain you actually weaken yourself. You generate feelings in yourself of inferiority and inadequacy. You feel angry and resentful. You feel negative and unsure. Your level of self-confidence and self-respect actually declines as you complain about anything to someone else. You hurt yourself by complaining much more than you hurt the target of the complaints, who you may not affect at all.

Remain Nondefensive

As Henry Ford II once said, "Never complain, never explain." One of the hallmarks of fully functioning people, according to the psychologist William Glasser, is that they are "nondefensive." They feel no need to complain and no need to explain themselves to other people.

I once made the mistake of complaining about something my son was doing. He looked at me and listened patiently while I went on. When I stopped, he looked me in the eye and said, "And your point is?"

As far as he was concerned, I could complain all I wanted. But it was going to have no effect on him or on what he had decided to do. He refused to be affected by my remarks, and I was proud of him for it.

If you are not happy about something, as the manager, you are entitled to bring it to the attention of the other person. You are responsible for putting it on the table and discussing it. If you are not happy with a behavior or an outcome, your job is to actively intervene to improve or correct the situation. But you do this by being honest and objective about the gap that exists between what you expected and what has actually happened. You then invite ideas and input on how you and the other person or persons can solve the problem or improve the situation. But you never complain.

No More Condemnation

The third behavior that you can stop is that of condemning anyone, for any reason, either inside or outside of your company. When you condemn other people, usually in private, you demoralize the listener, and the person you are talking about will hear about it almost immediately. When you condemn people *outside* the company, someone will eventually tell them what you have said, usually in a distorted version, and it will come back to haunt you. This seems to be a law of nature, and completely unavoidable.

These recommendations are equally as important when you are talking about competitors or customers in the marketplace. Never criticize your competitors. Admire them if they are more successful in some areas than you are, and then look for ways to produce even better products and services than they do, and find ways to sell them even more effectively. Never condemn people or businesses for any reason. Instead, use that same amount of mental energy to find solutions and to resolve the problems that led to your unhappiness with the situation in the first place.

The Six *A*'s of Self-Esteem

People have deep subconscious needs, and the deepest need of all, the core emotional need of the human being, is for self-esteem. It is to feel respected and worthwhile. It is to be liked and valued by the boss, the person with the most influence over the employee's work and income. The deepest need is to feel *important*.

There are several ways you can satisfy this deep subconscious need for self-esteem and personal importance. They all start with the letter *A*. The first is acceptance.

Practicing Unconditional *Acceptance*

From infancy, each person has a deep, unconscious need to be unconditionally accepted by the most important people in his or her life. When a person is accepted by others, she feels safe and secure. She feels unafraid and confident. She feels that she can express herself openly and honestly.

Sociologists say that lack of acceptance, or *rejection* by individuals or society at large, is the main cause of many problems with disaffected groups in our society. People who display antisocial behaviors are somehow trying to gain the acceptance of other people who do not approve of them currently.

The greatest gift you can give to a child is the gift of unconditional love. No matter what your child ever does or says, you love that child completely. Your love is not negotiable. It is a fixed amount, and that amount is 100 percent. There is nothing that gives a child greater confidence and security than knowing that she is totally and unconditionally accepted by the most important people in her life. It establishes a mental and emotional foundation upon which the child can grow into a happy, healthy self-confident adult.

Smile at People

If all you did was to continually express unconditional acceptance to each person you meet, both at home and at your workplace, you would soon be one of the most popular people in your world. And how do you express unconditional acceptance? Simple. Just *smile.*

It takes far fewer muscles to smile than to frown. When you smile at another person—a warm, genuine smile—you tell that other person that he is attractive, pleasant, likable, safe, and secure in your estimation. A single smile is so powerful that it can often transform people, jolting them from negativity and preoccupation to optimism and happiness in a single moment.

Smiles are so powerful that many long-term marriages and relationships have begun with a single smile shared across a room. You've heard people say that "when our eyes met, we both knew that we were meant for each other."

Enjoy the Payoff

There is a big payoff when you smile at people. When you smile, the physical action releases endorphins in your brain. Endorphins are called nature's "happy drug." They make you feel happy. They improve your sense of well-being and unlock your creativity. When you smile, you feel and act in a more personable way to everyone around you. The most popular and influential people in most situations are those who genuinely smile at others when they meet them and greet them.

Appreciating People for What They Do

The second *A* of building self-esteem is appreciation. People love to be appreciated for the things that they do and say.

Appreciation acknowledges their value and uniqueness. When you appreciate people, you raise their self-esteem, increase their self-confidence, and improve their self-image. The more you appreciate someone for something, the more likely that person will do it again, and do it even better next time, so that the individual can earn even more appreciation than before. The need for appreciation is a bottomless well that can never be filled.

The simplest way to express appreciation is to simply say "thank you" for anything and everything that people do that is helpful or positive in any way. Like smiling, speaking the words "thank you" releases endorphins in your brain, and those words trigger the release of endorphins in the brains of others, too, when they hear them. When you thank people for little things, they will strive to please you even more in the performance of bigger tasks.

A Traveler's Tale

Some years ago, a friend of mine who was traveling to the Far East for an extended business trip called me and asked if I had any advice for him that would help him get along better with the different people in different countries he would be meeting. Having traveled in those countries extensively, I gave him a single piece of advice: "Learn the words *please* and *thank you* in each country and in each language. Say them repeatedly and smile each time you say them. This simple gesture on your part will separate you from the majority of Westerners who go through the airports, hotels, and restaurants of Asian cities."

After two months of travel in several countries, he wrote to me and told me that it was the best advice he had ever received. He practiced those words wherever he went and was genuinely astonished at how kind and helpful people were to him, even in complex or difficult situations. He said this advice should be contained within the front page of every guidebook to every country ever published.

When you appreciate other people, at home or at work—or even outside of work—for anything that they do, you are recognizing their value as human beings. You are singling them out for a specific behavior and emotionally rewarding them for a particular effort. Just like your mother told you, the words *please* and *thank you* are like lubricants that grease the moving parts of human interaction.

Becoming an *Agreeable* Person

When you become a genuinely positive and cheerful manager, your general attitude will spread out from you, like a warm light, and fill the entire workplace. You will create an environment where people are relaxed and happy and feel good about themselves and their work. The third *A* for building self-esteem is *agreeableness.*

When people are asked to describe the companies that they prefer to do business with, and the people in those companies who they like the most, the word that they most use to describe them both always seems to be the word *nice.* Ask people why they buy from that company or shop at that store and they'll say, "Well, I could go somewhere else, but they are such nice people."

When people are asked to define the word *nice,* the most common definition is "cheerful." Nice people tend to be cheerful most of the time. Whenever you meet them, they are positive, pleasant, and appear happy to see you. They make you feel important and valuable, connecting with you on an emotional level. By being nice to you, they predispose you to want to do business with them again and again.

Another definition of what it means to be nice is "agree-able." Because of the unconscious fears of failure and rejection learned in childhood, most people like to deal with pleasant people who are friendly and agreeable most of the time. They don't want to fight or argue when they make a point or express their ideas. Agreeability is a wonderful lubricant to human conversation and interaction.

I have several friends in business with whom I have worked for ten, twenty, and even thirty years. In retrospect, I can say that we have never had an argument or disagreement. We have been through many complex and expensive business transactions, some of which were successful and some of which were not successful at all. We have had hundreds of hours of discussion and negotiation. But we have never had a disagreement.

Disagree Without Being Disagreeable

One of the keys to success in adult life is to disagree without being disagreeable. Everyone is entitled to a different point of view. Everyone brings different perspectives to the same event, even with the same facts. But there is never any need to be unpleasant or to try to dominate the other person with your arguments. You have heard it said that "a man convinced against his will is of the same opinion still."

The most successful people in business tend to be tactful and diplomatic in their discussions with others. They consciously and deliberately avoid doing or saying anything that would irritate or antagonize the other person, especially in a negotiation. Instead, they come off as agreeable and pleasant virtually all the time.

What if you and another person are in a situation where you both have differing viewpoints? What if the other person is, in your opinion, completely wrong in the position that he has taken? What if there is no way that you can go along with what someone else wants you to do based on your knowledge and understanding of the situation?

Again, you can disagree without being disagreeable. One way to deal with different viewpoints is to get complete control of your ego and try to put yourself in the place of the other person. Instead of arguing, when a person brings up a contentious or even an erroneous point, simply ask, "Why do you say that?"

Another way to disagree without being disagreeable is for you to use *third-party disagreement*. When someone says something contentious, and with which you disagree, you put your argument into the mouth of a nonpresent third party. For example, "That is an interesting idea. But if one of our customers [a third party] were to ask why we are making this change, how would you explain it to them?"

Harold Geneen, the onetime head of ITT, once said that "the biggest problem in business is not alcoholism; it is *egoism*." As soon as people take a position of any kind, right or wrong, they usually feel ego bound to defend their position against all challenges. Even if they are dead wrong, the more they defend their position, the more entrenched they become in their point of view, and the more difficult it is for them to change their minds.

But when you put the argument into the mouth of a straw man, someone who is not there, it is much easier for a person to climb down from an untenable position. Their ego is not involved when they are considering the opinions of a third party.

Resolve to Be Charming

My friend Ron Arden and I wrote a book called *The Power of Charm*. After years of research and experience, we mutually discovered that people who are described as "charming" are vastly more effective in influence and persuasion than people who are considered to be argumentative or abrasive.

If you want to come across as charming, be pleasant and polite, and ask questions rather than make statements. Then listen with great interest and attentiveness to the other person when he speaks.

A good strategy is for you to resolve in advance that you are going to be a charming person in every situation. Decide that you are going to be calm, friendly, and relaxed. You will be positive, pleasant, and agreeable. You'll be the kind of person that others enjoy talking to and being around. The more you can make other people feel good about themselves, no matter what positions they have taken, the more open they are to being influenced by you to change their minds in a direction of your own choosing. Try it and see if it doesn't work for you.

Expressing *Admiration* Regularly

Your goal is to raise the self-esteem of other people by making them feel important. And one of the very best ways to make people feel important and valuable is to *admire* them. Admiration is the fourth *A* of self-esteem. You can express your admiration for other people's possessions, their qualities, and their accomplishments. "Everybody likes a compliment," Abraham Lincoln once wrote.

You should always look for ways to compliment other people on any possessions they have about their persons, both in their personal and in their work life. Most people spend a good deal of time thinking about the things that they purchase for their homes or business, the clothes they wear, the accessories that they use, the cars they drive, the books they read. Whenever you deliberately pick out and notice something that a person has acquired and express admiration for it, you immediately make that person feel valuable and happy.

There Are No Limits

Compliment people on their clothes and accessories. Compliment them on their grooming. Compliment them on their ties, shoes, dresses, hairstyles, and briefcases. Whenever you notice something new or different about a person that catches your eye, immediately stop and tell the person. Say, "That is a beautiful tie," or "That is a lovely dress." Admire that "good-looking briefcase." Comment on "what a remarkable cell phone" the person is carrying, or on "the beautiful car" someone drives.

When you go into a person's office, it may be accessorized with pictures and possessions that are personal and individual to that person. Take a moment or two to notice what is important to the other person and then deliver a compliment. If you see a photograph, ask who the people are in the photo, and compliment those people in the picture for looking happy or attractive or for apparently having a good time.

When you go into an executive's office, notice the graduation certificate on the wall, the trophies on the shelves, the books in the bookcases, and the business tools that the individual uses. Take a few moments to observe carefully and then say something like, "That is a beautiful diploma. You must be very proud of that degree," or "That is a great-looking trophy. How did you win it?"

The moment that you take the time to compliment someone on something that is personal and unique, that person immediately sees you in a different light and becomes open to your influence. Any resistance that other people might have diminishes dramatically when you hand them a compliment. By complimenting them, you raise their self-esteem and make them feel good about themselves, so they immediately like you and are more open to cooperating with you.

Give *Approval* on Every Occasion

Expressing approval—the fifth *A*—is one of the most powerful ways of all to raise self-esteem and to make people feel more important. In fact, self-esteem is equated with the degree to which people feel that they are praiseworthy.

Whenever you praise and approve of another person, you satisfy one of the deepest emotional needs of people. Praise and approbation for any kind of effort or accomplishment makes people feel happy about themselves. They feel more valuable and important. People's self-esteem goes up and their self-image improves. And the more you praise people for what they do, the more likely they are to repeat the behavior that earned the praise in the first place.

Practice Praise to Encourage Behaviors

One of the things we know about the power of praise is that it must be done deliberately and intelligently for maximum impact. For example, if you want people to develop a positive behavior, each time they demonstrate that behavior you should go out of your way to notice it and praise them for it.

Some people regularly come late to meetings; but instead of criticizing them for their lateness, you should praise them when they come on time. "Thanks for being on time; you're presence here is really important."

When you praise people repeatedly for a positive behavior, they will eventually, as Freud said, "start moving from pain to pleasure." They will start engaging in the positive behavior more and more, and eventually they will drop the negative behavior completely.

Praise Immediately

When you praise people for something they have done, always do it immediately, right after the positive performance. When you make your praise immediate, it has the highest impact on influencing the other person to repeat that behavior. If a person works hard to complete a project on schedule, it does little good to praise that person several weeks later for her extra efforts. If someone works hard and completes a project late in the evening, and you phone him even later to thank him for getting the project completed, it has an enormous impact on that worker's future behaviors.

Practice Praise Everywhere

Once upon a time, my wife and I went out to dinner to an expensive restaurant. The hostess was not a particularly pleasant woman. As often happens, she led us to a table near the kitchen doors. As I always do, I scanned the room and picked out a table that was located in a better place and asked her for that table instead.

She was very snippy. "That table is no good," she said. "The waiter for that table is Henry, and he is the worst waiter in this restaurant." We politely assured her that we would take our chances and that we would prefer to sit at the better table. She seated us peremptorily, dropped the menus on the table, and stomped away.

When the waiter came to the table and asked if he could help us, I said, "Is your name Henry?"

"Yes, it is," he said.

"Well, we're in luck," I said. "Some friends of mine had dinner here last week and they said that you are the best waiter in this restaurant. We are really happy that you are going to be taking care of us."

Henry was flabbergasted. He asked, "Who was it? Who said that about me?"

I said I couldn't remember the name right offhand, but he made it very clear that Henry was the best waiter in this restaurant.

Here is a tough question for you: What kind of service do you think we got for the rest of the evening? The service was excellent in every respect, of course. Henry was pleasant, positive, attentive, and really enjoyed taking care of us. When I left, I mentioned to the hostess, in passing, that Henry was one of the best waiters that I had ever seen. She looked like she had just sucked a lemon.

Build People Up

Winston Churchill said, "If you want a person to demonstrate a virtue, impute that virtue to him in advance."

When you approve of a person's potential behavior or performance, in advance, you set up a force field of positive energy that motivates that person to do an even better job so as not to disappoint you.

When my son David was young, he was a bit shy and afraid of trying and failing at something new. I soon began telling him, "I know something about you; you never give up." I repeated this regularly. "David, you never give up!"

It worked. Over the next few weeks, he became more resolute and determined. Once he started something, he would see it through. The idea of quitting became foreign to him. As an adult today, he is almost completely unafraid, and he never quits at anything. He says to me, "I know something about myself; I never give up."

Give Praise Publicly

Here is another way to use the power of approval to great effect: Praise people in front of others. If your employees are doing a good job, take them to your boss, or the most senior person you can find, and "brag on them" to the other person. Make sure your employees hear you telling the senior person what a great job they just did. Explain the difficulties of the job and the intricacies of the performance. Build it up. Make a big deal of it. Let your employees bask in your approval. They will remember the experience for a long time.

Another way to express approval is to do it at your regular staff meetings. Before you start on the agenda, single out one or more people who have done something worthwhile since the last meeting. Itemize and explain in as much detail as possible what they did, how they did it, and how important it was. Explain the results that they got. And then lead a round of applause for the person who has just done a good job.

When you praise people in front of others, either as individuals or as a group, they will remember it for a long time, even years. More than that, they will strive to repeat the performance so that they can earn more approval in the future. When you raise people's self-esteem with regular approval, you make them feel wonderful about themselves, and motivate them to perform at ever higher levels.

Pay *Attention* to Them

Perhaps the most powerful of all techniques to make people feel important is to listen *attentively* to them when they talk to you. Learning and practicing this behavior until it becomes a habit can do more to improve your relationships at work and at home than perhaps any other single behavior. Paying attention to people is the sixth and final *A* of building self-esteem.

Listening is an essential management skill. You always listen to people you *value*, who you feel are important. You

listen when your boss speaks to you. You listen when someone you look up to and respect speaks. The more important
the other person is, the more you hang on every word, and
the more influenced you are by what that person says.

On the other hand, you always ignore what you don't
value. To put it another way, when you ignore other people
you *devalue* them, in their own eyes and in the eyes of other
people around them.

Let Them Talk

One of the biggest mistakes that managers make is that they
dominate the conversation. They talk too much. They interrupt people and complete their sentences. They ignore what
people have said and rush in to make their own points. They
override or even dismiss the arguments of others because
they are in a position of control and they have the power to
do it.

But every time you withhold your attention from others
when they are talking, ignoring them, you make them feel
less valued and unimportant. If you do this to someone in the
presence of others, you convey to the others that the person
speaking is of no importance. Not only that, but the other
people start to think that they are of little importance as well.
You start to create a negative downward spiral that can lead
to unhappiness and disaffection in the workplace.

When I hold my staff meetings, every person on the staff
is an agenda item. We go down the list and each person is
invited to bring everyone else up to date with what he is
doing, the problems he is facing, and what he is working on
for the future.

The Great Awakening

As a young manager, I would use staff meetings as an opportunity to hold forth with my own fascinating ideas, opinions,

insights, and advice. Other people seldom had a chance to speak. Eventually, people would sit quietly at the staff meetings, give a one- or two-word answer when they were called upon, and then leave the room quietly when the staff meeting was over.

It eventually dawned on me that I was abusing my position. Not only that, I was wasting the time of my staff and diminishing their effectiveness in their jobs. I decided to do an about-turn and instead of interrupting, I began saying less and paying much closer attention when other people spoke.

Now, whenever someone is speaking, I put everything aside, lean forward, and listen attentively to the person who is speaking. I nod, smile, and encourage staff members to continue to express themselves. Often I take notes and then ask questions, to get them to expand on what they just said. When people mention something they have done, I always compliment them and praise them in front of the other people.

As a result of this paying careful attention to each person, everyone is eager to get a chance to speak and share their experiences and ideas with the others. They have an "I can hardly wait" attitude. At the end of each staff meeting, everybody is happy and full of energy. They are all smiling, laughing, and talking with each other. They are all energized and eager to get back to work.

Every executive who has started using this style of conducting staff meetings has been astonished at the improvement in motivation, morale, and energy of their team members. And all it takes is a decision on your part to withhold your own fascinating commentary and instead focus in on and listen attentively to your staff members when they speak.

Four Keys to Effective Listening

There are four keys to effective listening. They have remained the same from time immemorial. No matter how many books and articles you read on effective listening, they all boil down to these four techniques:

1. *Listen attentively.* Listen without interruptions. Lean forward, face the person speaking directly, nod, smile, and be agreeable. When you nod and smile, you encourage people to keep speaking and to expand on what they are saying.

Attentive listening is a very powerful self-esteem builder. When people are listened to attentively by someone else, especially by someone important, their galvanic skin response increases—they may blush or perspire—their self-esteem goes up, their brain releases endorphins, and they feel happy and important. Their self-image improves and they feel more valuable.

Initially, it takes tremendous discipline to listen attentively, without interrupting someone who is speaking. But over time, as you notice the positive benefits of attentive listening, you will practice it more and more.

2. *Pause before replying.* It was well said that "most conversation is just waiting." In most cases, the people you think are listening are not really listening at all. They are preparing their remarks and getting ready for what they are going to say when the other person takes a breath. They then jump in with their own comments, largely ignoring anything the other person has just said. You want to break this bad habit. So, instead, make it a habit to *pause* for three to five seconds before replying. In this three- to five-second pause (or longer if warranted), you get three benefits:

■ You avoid the risk of interrupting the speaker if she is just reorganizing her thoughts before continuing.

■ You show the speaker that you are carefully considering what he has just said. This conveys that you value what was said, and by extension, you value the person, his thinking, and his words.

■ When you pause, you actually hear the other person at a deeper level. You get more of the actual message that is being sent by allowing a few seconds for the message to sink in. As Peter Drucker said, "The important thing in conversation is not what is being said, but what is being left unsaid."

3. *Ask questions for clarification.* Instead of jumping in with your own ideas or opinions, pause, take a deep breath, and ask a question, such as "How do you mean?" or "What do you mean, exactly?"

Remember, the person who asks questions has *control*. By taking a few seconds and asking a question to encourage the speaker to elaborate on her remarks, you control the conversation. When you ask questions, you also get an opportunity to listen again, more attentively. By asking questions, you get a chance to further build up the feeling of self-esteem and importance of the other person.

Most of all, remember the rule: "Listening builds trust." The more closely you listen to other people, the more they trust you, and the more open they are to being influenced and persuaded by you. *Telling* is not selling.

The more questions you ask, and the more attentively you listen to the answers, the more the other person will like you, trust you, believe you, and be open to you. On the other hand, the more you talk, interrupt, and jump in with your own comments, the more irritated and frustrated others will become, and the less open they will be to any suggestion you might make.

4. *Feed it back in your own words.* This is the real "acid test" of listening. When you can briefly summarize what the other person has just said, in your own words, and feed it back to him, you are telling the speaker that you were genuinely listening.

Most people will nod and smile, like the toy dog in the back of the car, when listening to someone else, but it's even more important that you thoughtfully reflect back what was just said. Then, when that person agrees and says, "That's it! That's what I meant," you know that person knows you were *really* listening.

Become More Conscious of Your Words

The best news is that everything explained in this chapter is behavior that you probably practice occasionally. The only question is: "How *often* do you practice this behavior with your staff?"

If you give yourself a grade from 1 to 10 on each self-esteem-building behavior, you have a benchmark from which to start. Wherever you give yourself the lowest grade is probably a good place to begin.

You don't have to change your behavior completely in any area. Just make a decision to raise your score by one or two points in one behavior over the next few days or weeks. As you review these ideas, imagine how you would treat your staff if you were already excellent in any one of these areas.

When you create a clear mental picture of yourself smiling, thanking people, being more agreeable, expressing admiration and approval, and paying close attention to them when they speak, you preprogram your subconscious mind to behave that way when you are interacting with each and every member of your team.

You have heard of the 80/20 rule. This rule says that 20 percent of what you do accounts for 80 percent of the results of everything you do. In working with your team, 20 percent of your behaviors account for 80 percent of the impact that you have on others, and those behaviors consist of the ways that you "make others feel important."

When you can make everyone in your company feel important, you will make a quantum leap forward in becoming an outstanding manager and get increasingly better results from every person who reports to you.

Action Exercises

1. Resolve today to eliminate criticizing, complaining, and condemning from your vocabulary, and from your workplace.

2. The next time there is a problem or misunderstanding of any kind, immediately focus on the future, on the solution, and on what can be done to improve the situation, rather than focusing on "who did what."

3. Each day when you go to the office, make it a practice to go around and smile at everyone before you begin your workday.

4. Make it a habit of thanking people for everything they do, large or small.

5. Take every occasion to praise people for every accomplishment, personally, by e-mail or by phone.

6. Admire people for their appearance and their accomplishments, and compliment each person on a regular basis.

7. Listen to your staff members attentively when they want to talk. Stop what you are doing, turn off your phone, put your papers away, and just focus on their words.

CHAPTER FIVE

Drive Out Fear

"What lies behind us, and what lies before us,
are tiny matters compared to what lies within us."

—RALPH WALDO EMERSON

The biggest single obstacle to success, happiness, performance, and productivity in any area of your life is contained in
fears of all kinds.

Fear is and always has been the greatest enemy of man-
kind. More personalities are undermined and destroyed by
fear than by any other factor. More relationships are hurt by
fear than anything else, however it is manifested. More psy-
chosomatic illnesses are caused by fears than by any other
single factor. The minimization and elimination of fear is the
key to becoming a fully functioning, happy, self-actualizing
human being.

One of the most important recommendations of W. Ed-
wards Deming, who revolutionized Japanese quality control
in the 1960s and 1970s, was "drive out fear." He concluded

that the opposite of a fearful workplace is an atmosphere of innovation, creativity, spontaneity, higher energy, and increased productivity. In a work environment where no one is afraid of doing or trying new things, everyone focuses more and more on doing the job better and better.

A Great Place to Work

In the research into what makes a "great place to work," perhaps the most important single factor is *trust*. Trust exists when you can say, "I know I can make a mistake at work without being criticized or fired."

When people feel free to try new things in order to do the job more effectively, increase quality, and improve customer service, all of their time, attention, and energy is focused outward, toward getting the job done better.

As you recall, Abraham Maslow referred to self-esteem and self-actualization as "being needs." These are the needs that people have to fulfill their individual potential and become more and more of what they are truly capable of becoming. When you drive out fear, what emerges is the most productive person that the individual can possibly be.

In Frederick Herzberg's discussion about Theory X and Theory Y management, he differentiated between hygiene factors—such as good pay, good working conditions, and job security—and growth factors, which consist of interesting work, pleasant coworkers, and an environment that encouraged and rewarded the best qualities of the individual. In other words, a work environment where people were *unafraid* to do their very best, without fear of criticism or disapproval, was essential to bringing out the very best in people and releasing the untapped potential of each individual.

Everyone Is Afraid

The fact is that everyone is afraid, in many ways. Fears of any kind, however, large or small, conscious or unconscious, inhibit and paralyze action and performance. The instant that a fear pops into a person's mind, because of the need for safety and security described by Maslow, the individual immediately thinks in terms of minimizing or avoiding the fear situation rather than maximizing performance and effectiveness.

Sigmund Freud based much of his work on what he called "the pleasure principle." Freud said that almost everything that we do is to seek pleasure and avoid pain. We are constantly moving *away* from things that make us unhappy or afraid *toward* situations where we feel happier and better about ourselves. Put another way, we are constantly moving from *discomfort toward comfort.*

The Key to Sales

In business, for example, financial success and growth are largely determined by the ability of the company to sell its products and services to skeptical customers in a competitive market. Financial success is in direct proportion to your company's ability to get people to take action on your product or service offering.

Why does a person take an action of any kind? It is only when the individual feels that, by taking the action, he will move from a state of lesser satisfaction to a stage of greater satisfaction. Economists call this a state of "felt dissatisfaction." The individual must feel dissatisfied in his current situation before any purchasing action is possible. The potential customer must then see that purchasing your product or service will relieve this felt dissatisfaction and lead to a state of greater satisfaction. Only then can a purchasing decision take place.

In a competitive market, we do not try to create needs. We try to identify customers who already have an existing need or felt dissatisfaction, and then show them that our product or service will satisfy that need or relieve that dissatisfaction. Because of competition, we must then convince the prospective customer that, of all the choices available in the market to relieve that dissatisfaction, our product or service is the very best choice for this customer, all things considered.

Eliminating the Fears That Hold People Back

In the world of work, one of the most important jobs of the manager, in tapping into the almost unlimited potential of his people, is to drive out fear of all kinds from the workplace. To do this, you must first understand where these fears come from, starting in infancy, how they affect yourself personally, and what you can do to minimize fears in both yourself and others.

In strategic and personal planning and goal setting, there are four questions that you ask to start with:

1. Where are we now?
2. How did we get here?
3. Where do we want to be in the future?
4. How do we get there?

The next sections of this chapter deal with question number two: *How did we get here?* We'll focus on what we know about where fears come from and how to apply it to the world of management and commerce.

Tabula Rasa Theory

Eighteenth-century philosopher David Hume postulated that people come into the world as a "tabula rasa," a blank tablet in terms of what they can be as adults. Although each child is born with inherent talents, abilities, interests, leanings, and personal potentials, in terms of overall *personality,* each person is a blank slate.

When the child is born, he has no fears at all, except for the fears of falling and the fear of loud noises. All other fears that you have as an adult have been taught to you over time as you grew up. Fears had to be learned. They were not inborn or inherited. Fears are *acquired* ways of thinking and feeling about yourself and the world around you. The only power they have is the power you give them by believing in them.

Two Remarkable Qualities

Each child is born with two remarkable characteristics. First, the newborn child is completely *unafraid* (except for the two fears already mentioned: falling and loud sounds). The child will touch, taste, feel, and get into anything; a child will run out in traffic, climb ladders, grab knives, jump into swimming pools, and will often do things that threaten his life and well-being at an early age. The child is not afraid. The child has not yet learned that there are certain things that he might do that can be harmful or even fatal to him. This is expressed in the child's attitude, "I can! I can do anything!"

Most parents spend the first few years preventing their children from hurting or killing themselves in a variety of different ways. Every day, you read of stories where a parent became distracted for only a few seconds or minutes, and the child ran out into traffic or fell into a swimming pool and drowned. This is why parents, in most cases, never allow their children to be alone while they are growing up. The consequences of a simple childlike error can be too negative to consider.

The second quality that the newborn child has is that he is completely *spontaneous.* He has no inhibitions or reservations at all. He cries, laughs, wets his diapers whenever he wants, throws food, does what he wants, says what he wants, whenever he wants, with no restraints.

Every parent remembers the child sitting in his high chair throwing his food in all directions and laughing with delight. Parents spend an enormous amount of time cleaning up after their children during their early years. This attitude is expressed by the child as, "I don't have to! I don't have to do anything!"

Normal and Natural Ways of Thinking

As it happens, the normal and natural state of the fully functioning, emotionally healthy adult is to be both fearless and spontaneous. In fact, throughout our lives, we continually move away from the discomfort of fear toward the comfort of feeling completely happy and relaxed in our environment.

The very best times of your adult life are when you are with your family or friends and you can completely relax and let go, saying and doing whatever you want, knowing that you are completely loved and respected by everyone around you. You cannot make a mistake or do anything wrong. You can be yourself with no fears of judgment, disapproval, or criticism at all.

When Parents Try to Take Control

To minimize the discomfort and inconvenience that the child's unrestrained behavior causes for them, parents attempt to control their children from an early age. Parents are busy and preoccupied with their jobs, their friends, families, and external activities. They often make the unconscious decision that the fastest and easiest way to simplify their lives is to get their children "in line."

When my parents were growing up in the 1930s and 1940s, the most widely read books and articles on child raising taught that the job of the parent was to "break the will of the child." This advice gave rise to the expressions "Children are meant to be seen and not heard," and "Do what I say, not what I do." The idea was that children at an early age are a form of domestic animal, like a dog or a cat. They are to be supervised, monitored, and trained to practice proper behaviors that are convenient and acceptable to the parents, their *owners*. Many parents today still treat their children as they would treat a dog or a cat. They come home, exchange a few words, and then spend the evening watching television while their children float freely around the house.

When Parents Act Like Their Parents

Unless parents make a deliberate, conscious decision to change, they will tend to treat their children exactly the way they were treated when they were children growing up. If they had negative and critical parents, they will be negative and critical toward their children. Because they have no other frame of reference, this way of treating children will seem to them to be normal and natural. It is all that they have ever known or experienced.

In an attempt to stop their children from doing anything they want, the first word that parents begin to say to their children is the word "No!"

They say "No! Stop doing that! Get away from there!" and "Don't touch that!" These admonitions are often accompanied by loud, emotionally distraught voices and sometimes with the threat or reality of physical punishment. The parent delivers this reprimand "for the sake of the child." Parents believe, usually unthinkingly, that by admonishing and shouting at their child not to do potentially harmful things, they are actually helping the child to develop reason and perspective with regard to her behaviors.

The Child's Emotional Response

But children are 100 percent emotional during their formative years. They have no understanding of what is right or wrong, good or bad, dangerous or safe. They need love like roses need rain. Their greatest need is for safety, security, and unconditional love from their parents. When their parents become angry, short-tempered, and shout "No!" or "Stop!" at them, children only internalize *one* thing—the feeling that "every time I touch or try something new or different, Mom or Dad gets angry with me. It must be because I'm too small, too incapable, too incompetent, and unable to do anything well."

From an early age, as the result of being told "No" and "Stop doing that," the child feels inadequate and unable to try or do new or different things. The child soon internalizes the words "I can't! I can't! I can't!"

The First Big Fear

If the discouragement from the parents is severe enough, and continuous, the child soon develops the fear of failure, which is the biggest single obstacle to success, achievement, and happiness in adult life. The fear of failure is called an "inhibitive negative habit pattern" by psychologists. It is a feeling of inadequacy, inability, and incompetence.

In more severe cases, whenever the individual, as an

adult, is presented with the prospect of doing something new or different, she reacts like a deer in the headlights. Instead of thinking of the opportunity or potential in the new situation, she immediately thinks about the possibility of failure and the negative reaction that she will get from the people around her.

In adult life, the fear of inadequacy is one of the greatest of all obstacles to trying something new. "What if it doesn't work?" "What if I tried and failed?" "If I try and fail, they will get mad at me, criticize me, and disapprove of me." As a result, your sense of safety and security is disrupted.

The inhibitive negative habit patterns are experienced *physically* as well, down the front half of the body. For example, the first physical manifestation of the fear of failure, of making a mistake, is usually felt in the solar plexus, the body's nerve center in the pit of the stomach. Then, the heart starts beating faster and often the throat goes dry. When you are really afraid, your bladder goes loose and you have a need to run to the bathroom. Often, people get headaches and upset stomachs when they are afraid. The very idea of trying something new or different, where failure is possible, causes physical effects and ailments that can keep people awake at night, and even make them physically ill.

Eliminating the Fear of Failure

You can cancel out a negative thought by replacing it with a positive thought. Perhaps the most powerful way to eliminate the fear of failure and the feeling of "I can't, I can't" is to say the words, "I can do it. *I can do it!* I can do anything I put my mind to!"

When you repeat the words "I can do it" over and over, your fears of failure diminish and your feelings of confidence increase. When you say those magic words over and over, you begin to cancel out those negative messages from childhood and earlier experience. You start to become a new person. You begin to shape your own personality.

My parents, because of their own fears, always told me that I couldn't do anything, that I would lose my money or my time, or fail in some other way. They passed their deep fears of failure and insecurity on to me. I am still working on getting rid of those fears completely.

When Barbara and I had our four children, we resolved to reverse the messaging. The only words our children ever heard, whenever they contemplated doing something new or different, were, "You can do it! You can do anything you put your mind to." As a result, our children have all grown up with the complete conviction that they can succeed at anything they really want to do. The fear of failure seldom enters their thinking.

Neutralize the Fear

One of your key jobs as a manager is to neutralize the fear of failure, the inhibitive negative habit pattern, in the people you manage. You do this by telling people that there will be no downside to making a mistake. When you pass out an assignment, you encourage people to do their very best, and then you make it clear that if it doesn't work out, you will use it as a learning experience and move on.

It is interesting that *leaders* never talk of failure in anything they do. As far as leaders are concerned, there is no such thing as failure. Instead, they use words like "learning experience," or "interesting feedback," or "less-than-optimum outcome." But they never use the word *failure*. As far as leaders are concerned there is no such thing as a failure; there are only lessons. Since most things that you try don't work initially, and sometimes they don't work through several iterations, leaders just look upon a failure as a necessary and unavoidable part of business life.

Treat Failure as a Learning Experience

When someone has an assignment in my company and makes a mistake, drops the ball, or ends up costing us money of some kind (which is almost always the case), I encourage the person to first of all say, "I am responsible." Once people accept that they are responsible for what happened, they then have no need to defend themselves or make excuses. Once you accept responsibility, the problem, which has already occurred, becomes a dead issue.

The second thing I do is to ask the question, "What did we learn from this situation?" We can then discuss the mistake or problem as though it had happened to someone else in a different company. We come at the situation with as much neutrality as possible. We examine it from every side to see what we can learn from the mistake that will enable us to be smarter and make better decisions in the future.

Focus on the Future

One of the best ways to drive out fear when a person has made a mistake is to use language that moves beyond the present situation to "next time," "in the future," and "from now on." For instance, you can say, "*In the future,* when this happens why don't we do this rather than that?" Or, "The *next time* this happens or comes up let's do this or that to make sure we don't have this problem again." Or, "*From now on,* whenever we have this kind of a situation, why don't we do this or that to make sure that we minimize the risks and maximize the opportunities?"

The good news is that whenever you use these expressions, you neutralize any criticism and you focus everyone's attention on the future. When you criticize people for something that has happened in the past, something that cannot be changed, they have no choice but to feel angry, defensive, and afraid. They become negative and fearful. They resolve not to take another chance in the future. Instead, they decide that they will play it safe rather than take any risks. If criticism for mistakes is widespread in your organization, in no time at all, everyone learns that "if you want to get along, you had better go along." Don't try anything new.

Celebrate Mistakes

One of the best things that you can do to drive out the fear of failure is to actually celebrate mistakes. When somebody has made a mistake that has cost time or money, and you have discussed it with that person in a positive and constructive way, bring it up at your next staff meeting. In front of everyone, explain what happened, how it worked out, and how much the mistake cost. Then, lead a round of applause for the person who made the mistake.

You turn a mistake into a celebration by congratulating people for having taken the risk in the first place. Reassure everyone that mistakes are as natural as breathing. Everyone makes mistakes. The most important thing is that we learn from the mistakes so that we can capitalize on what we have learned in the future. This response and behavior on your part will have an enormous impact on building a fearless team of high-performance individuals.

The Fear of Rejection

The second major fear that children develop over time is the fear of criticism or rejection. Psychologists call it the "compulsive negative habit pattern." The child learns this set of fears when the parents, in an attempt to control the child's spontaneity, punish the child by withdrawing their love and approval. One psychologist said that "all problems in adult life stem back to 'love withheld' in childhood."

Children need love the same way they need oxygen. The deepest need of the vulnerable infant is for safety and security. The primary source of this safety and security is the love and approval of the parent. If this love and approval is withheld for any reason, for any period of time, the child soon becomes anxious and fearful.

The Earliest Experiences

When Barbara and I had our first child, we read more than thirty books on child raising. This immersion in how and why children behave the way they do at an early age was a lifesaver for us. One of the important things we read was that when infants cry in the night, it may be because they are hungry or because their diapers are wet. But in many cases, they are actually crying out to see how safe and secure they are in this new world.

The time between when they cry and when their parent comes to comfort and reassure them is the indicator of how safe they are. If they cry for any period of time, without someone coming to take care of them, they begin to feel afraid and insecure. This fear and insecurity gets programmed into their subconscious minds, and is often manifested as fear and insecurity when they become adults, years later. This is why you cannot give children too much love, comfort, safety, approval, and security in their formative years.

In the old school of thinking, people said, "Let the child cry. It makes them tough." However, what we have found is that children who are left to cry by themselves, alone in the night, grow up fearful, uncertain, insecure, timid, and needy for the reassurance and approval of others. Children whose immediate needs are attended to continually while they are young grow up with greater feelings of security, self-confidence, and the willingness to take risks because they are not afraid of losing the approval of the important people in their lives.

Manipulation and Control

As children grow up, parents consider many of their behaviors to be inconvenient or disruptive. Because parents, like everyone, seek the path of least resistance, they find the best way to manipulate and control their children is to be stern and disapproving whenever their children do anything that is inconvenient for the parent. The fastest and easiest way to control someone who is dependent upon you for love and approval is to *withdraw* that love and approval. Use it as a tool. Give it sparingly to get compliance with your wishes, and withdraw it quickly to manipulate the behavior of the other, in this case the child. This behavior is behind many problems in adult life.

As a result of the parent withdrawing or withholding their love and approval, the child becomes terrified at an unconscious level. Soon he begins thinking, "I am only safe, secure, and loved when I do what my parents want, what they approve of, what makes them happy, whatever it happens to be at the moment." Children then make the unconscious decision to please their parents at all times, and do whatever they want them to do at that moment. They start saying, "I have to! I have to! I have to please others!"

Hypersensitivity to Others

This compulsive negative habit pattern makes the child, and then the adolescent, and finally the adult, hypersensitive to the opinions of others. When children grow up constantly fearful of doing or saying anything that their parents may disapprove of, they soon become fearful of doing or saying anything that their peers at school may disapprove of. This is why teenagers are so preoccupied with the opinions of their peers, and often dress, talk, and behave the way they do. This is invariably an attempt to earn the unconditional acceptance and approval that has been withheld by their parents.

The greatest influence that you can have over your children, at all ages, is for you to be their primary source of love and approval. When a child knows that his parents love him unconditionally, no matter what mistakes he makes, the child then organizes his life to become the person and do the things that he feels his parents would most admire or approve of.

Driving Out Guilt

One of the most insidious and destructive negative emotions that develops when parents give and withhold their love in an attempt to manipulate and control their children is guilt. The child is made to feel guilty if she does anything that displeases her parents.

If the root words associated with guilt and fear of criticism are "I have to, I have to," then the canceling words are "I don't have to. I don't have to! I don't have to do anything that I don't want to do."

Both Barbara and I were raised in families dominated by what we call "negative religion," where feeling guilty and making other people feel guilty were fundamental parts of the teaching. When we had our children, we resolved to eliminate guilt from our family. We would never use it, never allow it to be used on our children, and never make our children feel that they "had to" do anything to earn our unconditional love and approval.

Aside from matters of personal safety when they were young, we have never demanded or insisted that our children do or not do anything. We have always told them that they are free to make their own decisions. We are always there to give our advice, if they ask for it, but whatever they decided to do, we would back them 100 percent.

The most amazing thing is that, with this unlimited degree of freedom, they have almost always made good decisions for themselves, and if they made a poor decision, they corrected it quickly. The best part is that they have grown up to be positive, happy, self-confident adults, never having experienced destructive criticism or guilt-throwing in their lives.

Being a Good Example

The interesting thing is that you do not need to lecture your children about what they should or shouldn't do. By simply being a good example to them, a role model, you are helping them to decide for themselves that earning the approval of the person who most approves of them, their parent, is more important than pleasing their peers. They will start to imitate you and copy your behaviors.

The self-actualizing person identified by Abraham Maslow has the quality of being sensitive to the opinions of others, but not overly concerned. As a form of politeness and social affability, self-actualizing people are thoughtful about how others think and feel, but they do not make decisions based on earning the approval of others. If other people like what they do or don't do, that is fine. If they don't, it is unfortunate, but not a matter for any serious concern. They go their own way.

When you raise children with high levels of self-esteem and self-confidence, they will have a due respect for the opinions of others, but they will not be overly concerned or influenced by what other people may say or think.

Creating High Levels of Freedom

In the world of work, the best thing you can do as a manager is to create an environment where people feel completely free to discuss, agree, disagree, argue, disapprove, and express their opinions clearly and openly, with no fear that you will turn on them and threaten their job security with anger or disapproval.

The best news is that this open, spontaneous, free exchange of ideas in a positive, dynamic workplace leads to the unleashing of the very best energies of everyone in the workplace. This stimulates innovation and creativity, improves decision making, keeps people focused on solutions rather than problems, and creates a positive spirit that causes people to enjoy their work and to give of their best.

Stop Justifying and Rationalizing

But the best way to eliminate fear and enable freedom is for you to stop justifying and rationalizing to yourself that someone is bad or to blame for a problem that has occurred. If you are always quick to criticize and assign blame, people will be afraid to try anything or to give you bad news.

The fact is that all of business life is a series of problems, large and small. Problems are never ending, like the waves of the ocean. In fact, as a manager, your true job title is problem solver. From the minute you start work to the minute you go home, your primary activity is to solve problems, overcome obstacles, and make decisions. In fact, if there were no problems to solve, the company would probably not need your services.

Even more, the better you get at solving problems, by focusing on solutions all the time, the bigger and more important problems you will be given to solve. Along with these bigger problems come greater responsibility, higher position, and better pay. The more you focus on solutions, the more solutions you will come up with. The more creative you will become. The more positive and constructive an influence you will be on everyone around you. By focusing on solutions, you soon become one of the most important people in your organization, the go-to person whenever something goes wrong. When you focus on solutions, you stop criticizing and start making progress.

Don't Blame Others

When people make mistakes, focus on the solution, on what can be done to fix the problem, rather than who did it and who is to blame. This focus is the mark of the superior leader.

One of my areas of interest is military history. After the failed attack on the third day at the Battle of Gettysburg during the Civil War, General George Pickett's charge was repulsed with enormous losses, leading to the loss of the battle by the South. This day was called the "high-water mark of the Confederacy." From that day on, the South was never able to recover its previous strength, and eventually Robert E. Lee surrendered the Southern armies to General Ulysses S. Grant at Appomattox courthouse.

At the end of Pickett's charge, as the broken Confederate forces reeled back from the battlefield, wounded and bleeding, General Lee rode forward to greet the retreating army. He said, "All this is my fault. I alone am responsible."

Countless mistakes were made in the course of the largest

single battle that has ever taken place in North America. But Lee never criticized any of his subordinates, no matter what mistakes they made. He always accepted responsibility. To this day, he is revered as one of the great generals in American history.

Jump ahead to June 6, 1944. After the largest seaborne invasion in human history, and many hours of fighting, the Allies landed victoriously in France, leading ultimately to the collapse and surrender of Germany in April 1945.

Draw a Lesson from the D-Day Landing

After the invasion, General Dwight D. Eisenhower, commander in chief of the Allied forces, showed his subordinates a note that he had written out to read to the press in the event that the Allied invasion had failed. It said, "The landing has failed. Our forces have been repulsed. We have not been successful in landing in France. I alone am responsible for all the decisions that led up to this invasion."

Two great leaders. One great response to a major defeat and a potential defeat. In each case, the commanders refused to blame anyone for any failure that had taken place under their command. They accepted responsibility and focused their attention, and the attention of others, on the next step.

Interestingly enough, after Eisenhower retired from his two terms as the president of the United States, he and his wife, Bess, moved away from Washington to live out their years at their farm, on a piece of land at the edge of the Gettysburg battlefield, not far from where Robert E. Lee ordered Pickett's charge and accepted full responsibility for its failure 100 years before.

Accept 100 Percent Responsibility

Here is an interesting discovery. Your mind can only hold one thought at a time. The Law of Substitution says that you can *replace* a negative thought with a positive thought. You can substitute one for the other. Whenever you have a negative situation, problem, or difficulty of any kind, you can switch your mind from the negative to the positive in one second.

The best and most powerful way to eliminate negative emotions of any kind is to replace the negative situation in your mind with the words "I am responsible!"

It is not possible to accept responsibility and to blame or be angry at the same time. One cancels out the other. When something goes wrong in your area of responsibility, remember that "the buck stops here." You are in charge. You are responsible. You can immediately seize mental control over any situation in your life by emphatically affirming and reaffirming the words "I am responsible."

Building a High-Responsibility Company

Once you have accepted responsibility for yourself and your situation, you then encourage others to accept responsibility for their jobs—and the results of those jobs. But delegation is not abdication. Even if you have assigned a job to another person, you are still responsible for the ultimate results. You are in charge. You are in the driver's seat. You are the leader. You cannot absolve yourself of the responsibility by blaming other people and becoming angry at them. You can only undermine the strength of your position and your credibility by blaming others.

Encourage your coworkers to accept responsibility in a positive way. Encourage your children to accept responsibility in a positive way. Be a role model. No matter what happens, always remind others that you are in charge ("I am responsible"), and that there will be no finger-pointing or passing on of blame in your organization.

Keep everyone focused on the solution, on what can be done immediately to solve the problem or to achieve the goal. Get people thinking in terms of the actions that they can take now in order to bring about a better future. When everyone accepts responsibility, focuses on the solution, and thinks about the future, everyone on your team will work together in greater harmony and perform at their best.

Lowering Fear in the Marketplace

The fears of failure and criticism are major reasons for success and failure in the marketplace as well. The number one reason that people do not buy a product or service is because of the perception of "risk." The prospect fears that she will not enjoy the promised benefit of the product or service, or not enjoy it more than the satisfaction or benefits offered by another product or service. The prospect is afraid of making the wrong choice among products.

The prospect may also be afraid that others will disapprove of the purchase. In sales and marketing, the fear of rejection or disapproval is a primary force that determines whether people buy or decline to buy a product or service.

In years of working in sales, I never fail to be amazed at how many people cannot make a buying decision, of any kind, until they have talked it over with someone else—sometimes with many other people. Often, prospective purchasers have to get the approval of the members of their family, their friends, their work group, and their relatives. They continually say, "Let me think it over," and then they think it over, and over, and over.

The major job of marketing and sales today is to first of all convince your prospects that they will be better off with your product or service than with any other use of the money, and then to back up that promise with guarantees, warrantees, and other assurances that take away the perceived risk in the purchase of the product or service. The prospects must be convinced they have made the right choice.

One of the most powerful forms of advertising is the use of celebrity testimonials, which are used to combat the fear of disapproval and rejection. With celebrity testimonials, people who are well known and respected by others speak well of a product or service. Their endorsement increases the likelihood of prospective customers buying that product or service because they feel their purchase decision will be approved by other people who know and like the celebrity.

Business success only occurs when you "drive out fear" from the mind and the heart of the prospective customer. When prospective customers have been brought to the point where they are totally unafraid of buying from you, the sale takes place automatically and easily. All successful companies have harnessed this understanding to their benefit, and it lies at the root of all successful businesses and business offerings.

Setting Your Goals Without Fear

One of the questions that we ask in our seminars is this: "What one great thing would you dare to dream if you knew you could not fail?" The purpose of this question is to get people to presuppose they have no fears of failure or rejection, and are absolutely guaranteed of success in anything they want, large or small. In that case, what one great goal would you set for yourself?

Sometimes we put the question this way: "If you had $20 million in the bank, and you could do or stop doing anything in your life, what changes would you make?"

It is astonishing what happens to people's thinking when they hear these questions. They immediately think of all the things that they would want to do or to have or to be. As they think about what they would do with their lives if they were guaranteed success and protected from failure, they are amazed at how large the role of fear plays in their lives. When they are asked to think about what they would want to do or have if they had no fears at all, they often see their lives and futures completely differently.

There is within each of us a deep desire to fulfill our potential and become everything that we are capable of becoming. When you feel that you are capable of doing and being far more than you are achieving today, the feeling of "frustrated potential" becomes a major cause of negative emotions, unhappiness, and diminished performance.

On the other hand, when we feel fully liberated, capable of achieving almost anything we put our minds to, our self-esteem goes up, our self-confidence improves, and our potential for accomplishment expands dramatically. It is the job of the manager to create the environment where people feel like this much of the time.

Your Biggest Job

Your biggest job as a manager, in creating a peak performance environment, is to drive out fear. The way you do it is to first of all refuse to criticize anyone for anything. Make it clear that "mistakes happen." If your staff makes a mistake, their first job is to accept responsibility, and their second job is to propose a solution, or at least the next step that you can take to fix the problem.

Everyone should know that no one will ever be criticized, punished, or fired for making mistakes or for disagreeing with the boss. In fact, one of the best measures of a high-performance workplace is the degree to which people feel free to question the boss and disagree with his ideas or decision. The greater freedom that people have to speak up and express themselves clearly, without fear of being criticized, the more positive and powerful your work environment will become.

Action Exercises

1. Resolve today to eliminate destructive criticism of all kinds from your vocabulary. Hold your tongue for twenty-one days until you develop new and constructive habits to replace the old ones.

2. Whenever you feel angry or upset about anything, immediately say to yourself, emphatically and repeatedly, "I am responsible!" until the negative emotion dies away, which it will.

3. Drive out fear of making mistakes; make it clear that "failure is only feedback," and that the only thing necessary is to minimize the damage and learn from the error.

4. Tell people that "You can do it!" Express complete confidence in them to do good work and achieve excellent results.

5. Refuse to express displeasure or disapproval when people do something that you had not expected. Instead, ask them questions and listen closely to their answers.

6. Be a role model to your staff. As Gandhi said, "Be the change you want to see in the world."

7. Encourage openness, honesty, and disagreement with and among your staff; make them feel free to speak up about anything that is on their minds.

CHAPTER SIX

Create That Winning Feeling

"Cherish your visions and your dreams,
as they are the children of your soul,
the blueprints of your ultimate achievement."

—NAPOLEON HILL

Because of the powerful needs for self-esteem and self-efficacy, each person has a deep-down need to perform well, to succeed, to get results, and to feel valuable and effective. In short, almost everyone wants to feel like a "winner." Of course, people want to satisfy their dependency needs by being part of a team and a company. But at the same time, they want even more to satisfy their *autonomy* needs, their needs for independence, by achieving results for which they are personally responsible and personally acknowledged. They want to be on a winning team, but they want to be seen as winners in their own right.

That Winning Feeling

How does a person come to feel like a winner? Simple: by winning! It is only when a person actually wins that she gets the emotional enjoyment and satisfaction of that "winning feeling." Your job as a manager is to structure the work in such a way that people feel like winners much of the time.

The opposite of winning is *losing*. People feel like losers when they feel that they aren't making progress, satisfying their superiors, doing their job well, or being acknowledged and respected by coworkers, or when they receive no feedback on their performance. In each or in all of these cases, people lose their motivation and enthusiasm for doing their job the best way they can.

Emotions do not exist in a vacuum. People always feel *something*. If they do not feel positive, like winners, they will feel negative, like a loser. Your team members will experience one emotion or the other. Your job is to ensure that the predominant emotional experience is that of success, of winning, of making a valuable contribution.

For a person to feel like a winner he must cross the finish line first. Smart managers are always creating finish lines, both for individuals and for teams. They arrange the finish lines in such a way that people are always crossing them at the front of the pack. They create numerous opportunities for people to feel like winners.

Joining the 100 Percent Club

When I was working as a speaker for IBM, company executives told me how they structured the awards for their sales team. At the beginning of each year, they set sales quotas for each salesperson based on his experience, ability, territory, and the amount that he had sold during the previous year.

This gave each salesperson an opportunity to hit a personal quota, even if the other salespeople had higher or lower quotas than he did.

IBM carefully structured these quotas so that 70 percent of the sales force could reach them if they worked hard and followed the plan. Of course, they would have to stretch, and do more than the average, but the sales quotas were attainable.

As a result, 70 percent of the sales team each year hit their quotas. As a reward, they became members of the "100 Percent Club." They received special lapel pins that they could wear for the entire following year. They were sent on special vacations, received bonuses, and were both hailed and praised by senior management for their valuable contributions to sales revenues over the course of the year.

At the same time, about 30 percent of the salespeople did not meet their quotas. These people were encouraged to get additional training, work smarter and more efficiently, increase their level of sales activity, and were assured that they would probably meet quota in the coming year.

A Positive Dynamic

The dynamic that the company set up made IBM one of the best sales organizations in the world. First, 70 percent of the salespeople felt like *winners* when they hit quota, and they continued to feel like winners many months into the next year. They liked the feeling, and as a result, they worked harder in the following year to be sure to meet and surpass quota once again. They liked being members of the 100 Percent Club. They liked the additional respect and esteem that they received from other people in IBM. They were motivated to repeat their past performance, and to win again and again.

The 30 percent of salespeople who did not reach quota, but in most cases had come quite close, were even more motivated to hit their quotas the following year. They too wanted to feel like winners. They too wanted the special praise and accolades enjoyed by the members of the 100 Percent Club. As a result, they were internally motivated and driven to work even harder and smarter the next year. This healthy competition among the sales force was so powerful that IBM eventually reached the point in the 1980s where it was making 80 percent of computer sales in the entire world.

Getting It Wrong

Another company that I worked with decided to emulate the IBM model. This company created its own 100 Percent Club. Only the company's leaders did it differently. Instead of setting the quotas so that 70 percent of the salespeople could meet them and enjoy the rewards and recognition of top salespeople, they decided to make the achievement of this goal much more difficult. They therefore set the sales quotas so high that only 30 percent of the sales force, the hardest working, most experienced, and most highly motivated, could hit their numbers.

At the end of the year they passed out awards to the 30 percent who had hit their sales quotas and encouraged the rest of the sales force to work even harder in the coming year so that they could join this elite group. But this incentive system had the *opposite* effect. Instead of 70 percent of the sales force being able to relish their achievement and feel like winners, this company had set up a system so that 70 percent of the sales force spent the entire year feeling like *losers.* Not only did their sales not increase the following year, but they decreased, and many competent salespeople resigned and went to work for other companies where their sales results would be more greatly appreciated and rewarded.

One of the most important things you do as a manager is to organize the work, the incentives, the rewards, recognition, bonuses, and prizes in such a way that the majority of your people can meet or exceed their targets. Like a teacher who arranges field day activities at an elementary school, you need to structure the work and incentive systems so that almost everybody on your team gets a prize of some kind.

Expecting the Best

In a multiyear study of the most effective methods of motivating employees, the human resources executives involved came to the conclusion that the most powerful single motivator of all was having "positive expectations." The more that the manager expresses positive expectations about the talents and abilities of his people, and the more that individuals confidently expect to be able to do the job in the right way and at the right time, the more positive and motivated they are to perform at their best.

The good news is that most people want to do a good job. What they need more than anything else is your leadership, guidance, and encouragement to make that possible for them. They need to work in a climate of clear, positive expectations, knowing exactly what you want, when you want it, to what standard of quality, and the very best way to get it done. It is your job to provide them with just such a work environment.

Bringing Up Winners

Let me tell you a story. When my wife and I had our first of four children, we studied child raising exhaustively and were eager to be excellent parents. I am sure that all parents feel the same way when they have their first child. We read the books and pamphlets, attended the courses and lectures, and buried ourselves in the minutiae of raising happy, healthy, self-confident children.

We soon came across the works of Maria Montessori, an Italian scholar and teacher who developed what is known today as the Montessori Method. As a teacher, she developed a series of profound insights into how children actually learn and develop in the very best and fastest way. She then experimented for years in developing her system, and finally formalized it so that it could be duplicated by other Montessori teachers and administrators throughout the world.

After we had done our research on the Montessori Method, we were sold. The books told us exactly how to find a "true" Montessori school, which we did. As soon as our daughter Christina was three years old, she began the three-year Montessori learning process.

A Process for Creating Winners

Here's how it works: Each day, the child is dropped off at school. The teachers greet all the children by name as they arrive, shake their hands, and treat them like young ladies or gentlemen. They are always courteous and respectful toward the children.

The children then go to their class, depending upon their age and level of development, and are taught to immediately take their places on *the line,* which is in fact a large round circle that is drawn in the middle of the classroom with room for each of the students to sit comfortably. The class and class activities begin and end throughout the day with a return to sitting on the circle before getting up to engage in the next exercise.

Based on age and experience, the children are then given

tasks to perform. At Montessori, this is called "the work." The children are encouraged to see each exercise as important. It may be coloring with crayons, drawing with paintbrushes, assembling and disassembling puzzles, creating artwork, or something else. In each case, there is a beginning, middle, and an end.

The Teacher as Guide

The job of the teacher is to guide the children into and through each task. At the end of the exercise, which is always age and skill appropriate for each child, the children return to the circle one by one. They discuss what they have done and receive positive feedback from the teacher. They then embark on the next exercise.

For the student, completing Montessori exercises is like climbing a winding spiral staircase. Over the course of the three years, the exercises become more complex and difficult, each one gauged to the individual growth rate of the child. By the end of the basic three years, Montessori children can read, write, do mathematics, operate a computer, play a musical instrument, speak parts of a foreign language, know enough geography to recognize the various states and countries of the world, and are fluent in several other subjects.

Creating That Winning Feeling

What is most impactful is that for three solid years, students have been starting, working on, and completing ever more difficult tasks. At the end of each completed task, they receive compliments and encouragement from their teacher. This makes them feel like winners. The teachers continually tell the students how proud they are of how well the students are doing. There is no pass or fail. There are no losers. Every child *wins,* over and over again, day after day, week after week, month after month, for three years.

Can you imagine how children begin to feel, and how they emerge from the Montessori experience? The answer is "extraordinary!" They have high levels of self-esteem and self-confidence. They are proud of themselves. They are self-responsible and have high levels of self-respect. They have positive self-images. They like themselves and they like others. They feel empowered and capable of doing anything that they put their minds to. In their key formative years, they have learned repeatedly, by design, that they are competent, capable, and absolutely excellent human beings.

Once, when we were walking in a shopping center with our children, and our children were talking eagerly with each other in between dodging away and coming back, looking at different things for sale, and asking questions, a woman stopped us and asked, "Are those Montessori children?"

It was at that point that we realized that we had accomplished something quite wonderful with our children. With the constant reinforcement at school, matched with the constant encouragement at home, our children had started their little lives feeling like winners. They still feel and act like that today.

Five Steps to Winning

There are five ingredients in the recipe of creating that winning feeling. When you structure individual and team jobs around these five items, you will release a continuous stream of energy and enthusiasm toward improvement and excellence.

Step 1. Clear Goals

You've heard it said that "you can't hit a target that you can't see." And the follow-up is, "If you don't know where you are going, any road will take you there."

Clear, specific, written, time-bounded goals are absolutely essential to creating the environment in which people can win and feel like winners. The 10/90 rule in goal setting says that the first 10 percent of the time that you spend developing absolute clarity about what is to be done will save you 90 percent of the time once you begin. It can also save you 90 percent of the mistakes, the costs, and the lost time of other people involved.

In both personal and business goal setting, you should use the SMART model of goal setting. SMART stands for:

S = Specific

M = Measureable

A = Achievable

R = Realistic

T = Time-bounded

A SMART goal is *specific*. It is perfectly clear to everyone who must be involved in its achievement. The goal is clear and unambiguous. Most of the problems that people have achieving goals stem from a lack of clarity in setting the goal in the first place.

A SMART goal is *measureable*. It can be defined in numerical or financial terms. It can be broken down into steps, each of which can be measured as well. The more clear the measures, the easier it is to focus and concentrate on achieving those numbers. A child can tell you how close you are to accomplishing the goal.

A SMART goal is *achievable*. It can be accomplished within the constraints of time, money, the external environment, the economy, the skills and abilities of the team members, and the other constraints that exist both inside and outside the company.

The goal to "double our sales" is not a goal at all. But a goal that says "We'll increase our sales by 7 percent a month, approximately 2 percent each week, over the next twelve months," is specific, measurable, and achievable, and it leads to an increase of 100 percent in sales over the next twelve months.

A SMART goal is *realistic*. It is within the bounds of reality and is something that people can develop a high level of confidence in achieving. Many goals are merely "aspirational." They do not reflect reality. They are more wishes and hopes than goals.

Finally, a SMART goal is *time-bounded*. When you have specific schedules for the attainment of each part of the goal, and the completion of the final task, it is much easier for people to achieve the goal on schedule.

Empires have fallen and companies have gone bankrupt because the goals, which may have been clear to the people at the top, were never fully understood by the people who were expected to carry them out.

Step 2. Concrete Measures

For a person to win, he has to know where the finish line is. He has to know how you define winning. He has to know exactly what he has to do to complete the task and cross the finish line. A marathon is 26.2 miles, an almost heartbreakingly long distance for a runner. But fortunately, the organizers of the marathon have posts or markers every mile, and sometimes every half mile, so that the runners can measure their progress in shorter, more achievable increments. The smaller and tighter the increments, the easier it is for the person to feel like a winner. It is the same at work. Each time that staff members achieve a mini-goal, they feel like a "mini-winner."

Milestone Management. In sales organizations, it used to be common to heap rewards on salespeople who made the big sales upon which the company was dependent for revenues and growth. But often, these big sales would take as much as a year or longer to complete. In between, the salesperson would be deprived of that winning feeling.

Today, sales organizations break the sale down into a series of milestones. The first milestone may be identifying an ideal prospect. The second milestone may be gathering information. The third milestone may be getting an appointment with a key decision maker. The fourth milestone may be identifying the need that the customer has that your product can satisfy. The fifth milestone could be assembling a presentation, and so on.

In top sales organizations they call this process "milestone management." Each week, the sales manager reviews the number of prospects who are at each stage of the sales process. Based on experience, they know how many of these prospects will eventually turn into paying customers, and the average size of each sale.

With this information, they can make fairly accurate sales projections on monthly, quarterly, and biannual bases. This process allows the sales organization to "manage by objectives" and keep people focused on doing one thing at a time. More important than anything, by focusing on the milestones, the salesperson gets that winning feeling at every step of the sales process. The closing of the sale is merely the final step where the total winning process is consummated.

When you assign people a large, multitask project that may take many months to complete, be sure to set up a series of milestones and benchmarks so that people can have short-term targets to aim at, and can continually generate the feeling of winning.

Step 3. The Success Experience

For a person to feel like a winner, he must *succeed* at the task. He must achieve the goal. He must fulfill the responsibility and get the result that he was tasked for. He must clearly win.

It is the job of the manager to help each person to have success experiences. If a person has been given a job that is too much for him, the job of the manager is to adjust the job, assign parts of it to someone else, and make it more manageable for the employee. The focus is always on making sure that, whatever job people have, they are capable of doing it successfully sooner or later.

When you start new employees, one of the best motivators is to give them a series of small jobs that are clearly within their experience and ability. Just like at Montessori schools, the starting and completion of small jobs builds up an emotional "head of steam" that raises the employees' self-esteem and increases their confidence in their ability to complete even larger jobs.

Step 4. Recognition for Achievement

Everybody needs to be recognized for their individual accomplishments by the people around them, and especially the people above them. Since your team members are internally motivated, it is often the anticipation of the recognition they will receive for the completion of a task that motivates them internally to "go the extra mile." As explained in previous chapters, positive recognition for an accomplishment raises people's self-esteem, improves their self-image, and motivates them to do even more and better in the future.

Step 5. Tangible and Intangible Rewards

This is the icing on the cake. You can only get by with offering praise and recognition for task completion for a limited amount of time. At some point, you must give some kind of reward to acknowledge superior results. If there are no rewards following extra efforts, people lose their enthusiasm and in their minds conclude, "What's the use? Even if I work hard and do a good job, I don't get any more than the other people around here who don't work as hard."

Rewards, however, can be tangible or intangible. A tangible reward is material or financial in some way. It may be a briefcase or a gift certificate. It may be a bonus or a pay increase. These rewards are some of the greatest motivators of all in the world of work and act as a continuous spur to better performance.

A Good Lesson. When I was a young manager, running my own business, whenever someone did a great job on a particular project, I would give the person an increase in pay. This practice soon came back to haunt me. The next time they did a good job, which was part of their job description anyway, they again wanted an increase in pay. Worse than that, so did everyone else when they did the job that they had been hired for. Soon, my payroll costs were getting out of control.

I soon learned that the best financial reward is a specific bonus tied to completion of a specific task. It is a onetime affair. It is not a permanent pay increase that goes on month after month. Short-term rewards and bonuses are just as motivating as long-term pay increases.

Rewards Other Than Money. Rewards can be intangible as well. An intangible reward can be something as simple as taking the person out to lunch to celebrate a success. It can be a bigger office or desk. It can be a new office chair or a new computer.

Another intangible reward is time off. When my staff members are doing a great job on a project, I tell them in advance that they need not come in on a Friday. I always give them time to plan their day off in advance, rather than telling them at the last minute.

Here's what happens: When you give people a day off as a reward, they will get all their work done before they leave and catch up quickly on their first day back. You will lose no productivity. The payoff to you and the company is a more motivated person who is eager to earn even more days off with pay, at no financial cost to you.

Another intangible reward is additional training. Many companies send their high performers to two- or three-day training programs locally or as an out-of-town business trip. This gives a double benefit. The individual learns how to be even more competent in achieving higher and more important goals in the future. The company develops an employee who is capable of contributing even greater value. It is a win-win for both parties.

There are many different ways to reward people, both tangible and intangible, for accomplishing goals that are above and beyond the call of duty. Some managers hand out small cash awards on the spot for accomplishments, even for ideas and suggestions. Others send flowers home to the spouse of the person who has just accomplished an important goal. You can give sports tickets, concert tickets, movie tickets, or even a gift certificate to a nice restaurant. The rewards you give to encourage top performance, and make people feel like winners, are limited only by your imagination.

Delegation Creates Success

People need to achieve measurable goals and be recognized and rewarded for their achievements to feel like winners. The more autonomy and responsibility they are given to achieve those goals, the more meaningful their success. It's one thing to be successful doing something for which you received detailed instructions from your boss. It's more satisfying to do something successfully when you had complete responsibility in figuring out how to do it.

This is where delegation comes in. Delegation is how you maximize the potential of your staff. The more and bigger tasks that you delegate to people, the more capable and competent they become, the stronger their self-confidence and self-efficacy, and the greater their value as a resource for your company.

The starting point of delegation is for you to think through the job in advance. Think through exactly what needs to be done and what the ideal result will look like.

Set standards of performance for the job and make them measurable and time-bounded. How will you know that the job has been done in an excellent fashion? If you could wave a magic wand and have this job done perfectly, what would the result look like?

Determine a schedule and a deadline for completion. When do you want it done? When do you need it to be done? When must it be done?

Selecting the Right Person for the Job

Once you have thought through the job clearly, you must look around and identify the right person to do the job. The experience level of the individual determines the actual method of delegation.

A new person, or an experienced person in a new task, has a *low experience level*. In this case, they require hands-on management. They must be shown how to do the job and supervised, step-by-step, to ensure that they do it on time and in the proper manner. You should never delegate an important task to an inexperienced person.

The second type of person has a *medium experience level* with a demonstrated ability to do the job. With this type of person you use a management-by-objectives approach. You discuss and agree clearly on the goal to be achieved and the task to be accomplished. You can even express your preference for exactly how the job is to be done. Then, you leave the individual alone to complete the task.

The third type of employee is one with a *high experience level*. This person has a demonstrated competence in the job and is probably better at performing the task than you are. In this case, your method of delegation involves easy interaction and conversation. You discuss and agree with the other person on exactly what needs to be done and ask what she needs from you to make it easy for her to do the job. Then, you get out of the way and let the employee get on with the work.

The Process of Effective Delegation

There are seven steps to effective delegation. When you follow these steps, in order, and delegate the task effectively, you set up the optimal conditions for the person to perform well, succeed, and feel like a winner.

1. *Select the right person for the job in the first place.* Match the requirements of the job to the skills of the person. Your selection of the right person in the first place will determine 80 percent or more of your success in getting the job done correctly, on schedule, and on budget.

2. *Delegate the whole task.* Having 100 percent responsibility for the completion of a task is a major motivator of performance.

3. *Delegate specific results and outcomes.* Make them measurable. What gets measured gets done.

4. *Delegate with participation and discussion.* There is a direct relationship between how much a person discusses the job with you before she begins and how committed she will be to doing the job well. Explain and agree on what is to be done and why.

Here is an important insight. People are either *visual* or *auditory.* Visual people need to see things written down. Auditory people can best understand things when they are discussed verbally. You should address both modalities when you delegate a particular task. Always have the person write down the task that you are discussing, as you discuss it. At the end of your discussion, ask the person to repeat back to you what the assignment is.

As a young manager and business owner, I would often delegate a task with discussion and agreement, and then go on my way confident that the task would be done as specified, and on time. I was continually frustrated to find that employees had not done the job that I had asked, or had not done it the way that I had asked. In fact, they had completely misunderstood what I was asking them to do in the first place. From then on, I began requiring that staff members feed back to me any assignments we have discussed, and you should do the same.

5. *Set clear deadlines and sub-deadlines for the completion of each task.* Don't leave it "hanging in the air." If it is a big task, set sub-deadlines for how much of the task is to be completed each week. If it is a one-week task, set interim deadlines for how much of the task is to be completed each day. The tighter your deadlines, the more likely the job is to be done on time.

6. *Delegate authority over the resources necessary to do the job.* Give the delegatee the time, money, assistance of other people, and whatever resources are necessary. Be clear and specific, especially with the amount of time available, both of the person and of the people you assign to that person. Be clear about the budget. Take nothing for granted.

7. *Once you have delegated the job, leave the subordinate alone.* Don't take the job back by interfering or offering to do parts of the job.

In a classic *Harvard Business Review* article, "Management Time: Who's Got the Monkey?" William Oncken describes the tendency for managers to become overloaded with jobs that they have delegated to others. He points out that employees are masters of *reverse delegation.* Partway through a job, they come back to the manager and ask if the manager can help them in some way, by getting some information or making a phone call. The manager, trying to be a good person, agrees to help out with a part of the job.

But here is what has happened. The person who is responsible for the *next* step in the job now owns the job. The monkey is now on his back. This employee can no longer work on the job. He has to wait until the manager has completed the next step before he begins again.

In no time, the subordinate becomes the manager and the manager becomes the subordinate. The subordinate drops by the manager's office and says, "How's it going on that task that you promised to do for me?"

From now on, when an employee comes to you and asks for your help on a part of the job, keep your hands behind you. Refuse to touch it. If the employee wants your advice, you instead ask, "What do *you* think we should do in this case?" Whatever the answer, agree and encourage the person to do that. With this approach, employees will learn soon enough. Don't take the job back once you have given it away.

Management by Exception

A good way to maximize efficiency in delegating is to practice "management by exception." With this method, you set clear goals, standards, and deadlines. Then, you only require reporting if there are exceptions or deviations from the agreed-upon schedule. As long as the employees are doing the job on schedule, they do not need to come back to you. It is only if there is a problem that they refer to you for your help.

Participative Management

One of the descriptions of a great place to work is that people feel "in the know." They feel like insiders, privy to everything that is going on within the company. They are continually told what is happening and how it will affect them.

Participative management is how you get people fully engaged in the company so that they feel that every success of the company is a personal success that applies to them as well. People have needs for independence, dependence, and interdependence. Participative management satisfies the deep need for interdependence. It makes people feel as if they are part of the whole organization, as if they can take personal ownership for the organization's success. For this approach to work, however, you must take time to explain everything that is going on and continually invite questions from people, individually and in your staff meetings, about changes and developments.

Continual Encouragement

Continually express positive expectations to your team members. Tell them that you have complete confidence in them doing their work and completing the tasks that have been assigned to them.

Give them constant encouragement. Tell them how well they are doing. Build them up with appreciation and approval. Give praise regularly. Catch them doing something right. Whenever you see employees doing anything that is a positive, mention it and praise them for it.

Perhaps the greatest contribution you can make to your company is to encourage your staff to feel like winners most of the time. If you want to create winners, you must create the conditions in which they can win. You must set up goals, standards, and finish lines. You must help them to cross the finish line, to be successful. You must then reinforce this success with praise, recognition, and rewards.

When you make people feel like winners, you are creating a peak performance environment that's full of people who will do the very best job they possibly can for you and your company.

Action Exercises

1. Make your people feel like winners by setting up the conditions in which they can win every day, with every job.

2. Describe each job clearly and have the staff member describe back to you exactly what you want him to do.

3. Set clear measures of accomplishment on each task, and on each part of the task. Make them clear to everyone.

4. Seek ways to recognize and reward excellent performance whenever it occurs.

5. Get people the additional resources that they need to do their jobs in an excellent fashion.

6. Give regular feedback on performance. People need to know how they are doing on a regular basis.

7. Hold weekly staff meetings and make each person an agenda item; allow all staff members to share what they are doing, their problems, and their plans for the days ahead.

CHAPTER SEVEN

Select the Right People

"The best executive is one who has sense enough to
pick good people to do what he wants them to do,
and self-restraint enough to keep from meddling
with them while they do it."

—THEODORE ROOSEVELT

All of your hard work and effort in building up people's self-esteem and self-image, as described in the preceding chapters, won't help you achieve your goals as a manager and a leader if those people are the wrong people for your organization in the first place.

Your job is not to find people and transform them into something that they are not already. Your job is to find good people and create an environment where they can perform at the highest levels possible for yourself and your business.

Your ability to select the right people for your team in the first place will account for 95 percent of your success as a manager or business owner. It is amazing how many managers hire people who are wrong for the job and then try to work around them, causing enormous frustration and disappointment for everyone.

In his book *Good to Great,* Jim Collins is famous for saying, "Get the right people on the bus. Get the wrong people off the bus. And then get the right people in the right seats on the bus." That, he says, is one of the seven keys to business success.

Everything starts and ends with having the right people in the right jobs at the right time. One difficult person or poor performer can sabotage the performance of the entire team. The previous chapter talked about creating an exciting vision for your business, especially for the kind of people you want to work with and for you. In this chapter, I want to share a few ideas that you can use to make better hiring choices throughout your career.

Peter Drucker said that "most hiring decisions do not work out over the long term." It seems that about one-third of the people that you hire will be excellent for their jobs. But one-third will be average, and the final third will be completely unacceptable. Your job is to improve on these odds and make better hiring decisions more often than the average manager.

Wrong Hiring Is Expensive

Making a wrong hire can be an expensive mistake, both for you and for your company. It costs between three and six times the person's annual salary if you hire someone and that person doesn't work out over time. Where do these numbers come from? They are made up of several factors:

- The number of hours that you and others have to invest to sort through candidates and find the right one to hire in the first place.

- The cost of training and integrating people into your activities before they are really capable of contributing any value to your business. This effort can take two or three months, or even longer.

- The salary and benefits that you pay people while they are learning how to do their job.

- The time and the cost of the supervision, and the salary and benefits of the supervisors, which have to be included.

- The low level of productivity from a new person that is almost unavoidable in the early months.

When a person works for you and leaves after six or twelve months, for whatever reason, 100 percent of these investments in that person are lost. They are gone forever. They are irretrievable. There is no value left.

Now, as a result of hiring the wrong person, you have to start the entire process over again. Again, it takes time and money. This is probably why the most profitable companies seem to be the ones that have the lowest levels of turnover. Companies at which there is high turnover, for whatever reason, tend to be less profitable than others.

The final loss has to do with employee morale. When there are high levels of turnover, people become demoralized. They started to work and interact with the new person, and suddenly that person is gone. They begin to wonder if their jobs are safe. They wonder if their management is competent. They wonder if there are fundamental problems with the company. They spend a lot of time talking and gossiping about the people who have come and gone. Productivity drops. When there is high turnover, there are lower levels of motivation and commitment. The whole company slows down.

Good People Are Free

On the other hand, good people are free. What this means is that good people, highly productive people who get along well with others, always contribute more to the company in value than the company pays them in salary and benefits. In fact, the basic rule is that workers should contribute three times their total costs in value of some kind to the business. Although this is hard to calculate for knowledge workers, technical workers, secretarial staff, and administrators, they too must contribute more than their cost or they end up becoming a net loss to the business.

There was a huge controversy in the newspapers in 2009 about a commodities trader in New York who was paid $100 million in bonuses by Citibank, even though Citibank was going through serious financial problems in 2008 and 2009. The politicians were outraged. How could anyone be worth $100 million a year?

The senior executives at Citibank patiently explained that this incredibly competent investment specialist was paid on the basis of performance. He received a percentage of profits that he generated for Citibank. In the year in question, he had generated more than $2 billion of net bottom-line profits to Citibank. His $100 million paycheck was the agreed-upon amount that he would receive for achieving these profit goals.

Hiring Begins with Dehiring

In many cases, hiring begins with *dehiring*. You often have to get the wrong people off the bus before you can start building a superb team of high performers.

It turns out that the most stressful event in a manager's life is being fired. The second most stressful event is firing someone else. The sad fact is that if you don't get some experience with the *latter*, you are going to get some experience with the *former*. If you don't get rid of the poor performers under you, the company will replace you with someone who will.

Peter Drucker said that "a manager who keeps an incompetent person in place is himself incompetent."

Throughout your career, one of the most important thinking tools that you can ever use is called "zero-based thinking." This concept comes from accounting. In zero-based accounting, the manager examines every expense every year, and often every quarter, and asks the question, "If we were not now spending this money in this way, would we still budget for it, knowing what we now know?" Instead of debating whether to increase or decrease a budget item, you ask whether you should be spending money in that area at all.

The best managers put their previous decisions on trial for their lives on a regular basis. They are always willing to revisit a previous decision, in any area of their business, based on the current situation and current information.

It takes tremendous courage to admit that you may have made a mistake. But it is all right. In times of turbulence and rapid change, you will make mistakes 70 percent of the time. The only question is: How long is it going to take you to admit it and begin making the necessary changes?

Applying Zero-Based Thinking

With your staff, the zero-based thinking question is, "Is there anyone working for me today who, knowing what I now know, I would not hire again if that person applied for the job again today?"

This is called a KWINK ("knowing what I now know") analysis. You can apply this tool to every single part of your business on a regular basis, but especially to the people part of your business. Think about each of the people reporting to you. Is there anyone who you would not hire back again today, knowing what you now know about that person's job performance? If there is, the next question is, "How do I get rid of this person, and how fast?"

What we have found is that if you would not hire this person back, knowing what you now know, it is too late to save the person. Now the issue becomes how long it's going to take you to do what you need to do.

How can you tell if you are in a zero-based thinking situation? The answer is simple. It is called "stress." Whenever you experience stress, frustration, anger, disappointment, or any ongoing feeling of negativity about one of your staff members, you should call a mental time-out and ask, "Would I hire this person back again today, if I had to do it over?"

Another way of phrasing the zero-based thinking question with regard to staff is, "Are there any employees working for me who, if they came to me and told me that they were leaving, I would not try to talk out of it?" Every manager has had the experience where he was wishing, in his heart of hearts, that a particular employee would just quit and go away. When it actually happens, the manager feels a great sense of relief.

Misplaced Compassion

Some managers keep poor performers in place because of a misplaced sense of loyalty or compassion. They fool themselves into believing that the reason that they do not let the person go is because they are kinder and gentler than other managers.

But this is merely self-delusion. The reason that you do not fire an inappropriate person is because of *cowardice.* You are simply afraid of the stress involved in letting someone go. It has nothing to do with compassion at all.

Here's an important point. When you have decided that you would not hire a person back again, knowing what you now know, this means that this person has no real future in your business. His days are numbered. It is only a matter of time before he leaves or is fired. The situation is not going to improve. It is too late.

The kindest thing that you can do as a manager, when you realize that this job is not going to work out for that person, is to *set him free.* When it is clear that the employee has no future in your company, don't tie up that person's life and keep him on the payroll. This simply holds people back from finding the job that is right for them, rather than the obviously wrong job they are doing at the moment.

No Guilt, No Blame

It has been said that a weakness is merely a strength, inappropriately applied. If someone is not doing the job properly, and obviously cannot do the job that you need to get done, it doesn't mean that the person is bad or evil for any reason. It simply means that there is a mismatch between what you need and what the other person has to offer. The sooner you identify that this mismatch exists, and let the person go, so he's free to find a more appropriate position, the better off both of you will be.

Use the KWINK analysis test with each member of your staff. Whenever you are unhappy or stressed for any reason because of one of your staff members, ask the question, "Would I hire this person back again if I had to do it over?" When you finally muster up the courage to follow through on your decision and let the person go, you will have the same feeling afterward that all managers come to realize: "I should have done this a long time ago!"

Once you have gotten the "wrong people off the bus," only then can you build a peak performance team that will enable you to fulfill your business destiny.

Choosing Winners

Many managers have never been trained in the employee selection process. Without warning, they find themselves in the position of hiring someone else to work with them. Instead of realizing that selecting a person is very much like selecting a mate in marriage, they approach the process in a random, haphazard fashion. As a result, especially in their earlier years, managers make mistake after mistake in hiring and placing people.

But this is not necessary. All the answers have been found. Tens of millions of people are selected and put into jobs every year. There are specific steps that you can take to dramatically increase the likelihood that you will pick the right person at the right time, at the right salary, to do the right job, and someone who will fit in ideally with the other people on your team. You don't need to reinvent the wheel.

Think on Paper

Start off by thinking on paper. There is something quite wonderful that takes place between the head and the hand. When you write something down (not type it out on the computer, but write it on paper) you clarify and better understand what it is that you are really looking for. The fact is that if you cannot describe the person you are looking for by putting it in writing, you probably do not understand what you want.

Once you begin to develop a clear idea of the person you

are looking for to do the specific job that needs to be done at this moment, you should discuss your thoughts with other people who will be involved. Ask for advice and ideas from the other members of your team. Get them involved and keep them involved in the selection process. You will be both surprised and delighted at the quality of ideas that your staff will give you, which will genuinely improve your ability to select the right person in the first place.

Take Your Time

In selecting and hiring, take your time. Fast hiring decisions are almost always bad hiring decisions. As the proverb says, "Make haste slowly."

Each time you think of hiring a new person, think through the job completely, as though it never existed before. Nowadays, a job description becomes obsolete before the ink dries on the paper. What was an essential skill or output responsibility for a job this year may be completely irrelevant by next year. In designing the job, imagine you are starting with a blank sheet of paper. Imagine that you have the ability to start over, including more of the things that you need today and deleting features of the job that are no longer important or relevant.

Start with Results

Start off by listing the exact *results* required of this job. A result is like a goal, in many respects. It is specific, measureable, and time-bounded. Especially, it is the sole responsibility of the individual who has this job. What will this new person be responsible for producing for your business or organization? Will she be completely responsible for the completion of specific tasks? Or will she be doing one part of a job while others are doing other parts of the same job?

If you think of your company or department as a factory, you can then view each person as someone on the production line who does a specific job. Almost like a bucket brigade, where a bucket gets passed from one person to another, in a business, people take the job that has been done by the person before them, perform their part of the job, and pass it on to the next person. Although this is an imperfect way of describing knowledge work, when you hire a person you are hiring units of production of a specific kind. You must be clear about what they are. Think on paper.

Measure Success

How will you measure success? The fact is that if you can't measure it, you can't manage it. How will you know that the job has been done in a satisfactory way? How will others be able to determine the quality of the work? You owe it both to yourself and to the new employee to be completely clear about what constitutes excellent performance. This is essential to creating a high-performance workplace.

Identifying Skills and Experience

What skills and experience will be necessary to do this job? Of all the skills that the ideal candidate would have, what are the most important skills? One of the smartest things you can do in your position is to hire people who have already developed the skills you need from their previous experience somewhere else. This is much better than you having to invest the time, trouble, and expense of teaching these skills yourself.

The Right Fit

What kind of *personality* will fit in best with you and your company? This is one of the most important questions of all.

For people to perform at their best, they must fit well with all the other people on the team. They must be able to work in harmony with your team members and to be both liked and respected by them.

Each company has its own personality. This starts from the top and filters down. "Birds of a feather flock together."

Some companies are established and conservative in their orientation. They move carefully and slowly and do not like people who rock the boat. Their belief is that "if you want to get along, you must go along."

Other companies—especially younger, high-tech companies—are more open, expressive, and entrepreneurial. They welcome spontaneity and creativity. They encourage debate and argument over products, processes, services, customers, and how to do each of them better.

Right Person, Wrong Company

During a seminar a woman came up to me to ask for my advice. As she explained her current job, she was obviously a bit frustrated. She said that she worked for a 100-year-old company. All the managers had been there for twenty and thirty years. Whenever she suggested what she thought were better or more creative ways to do the job, to make the product or serve the customer more efficiently, her managers made it clear that her suggestions were not welcome. They did not believe in rocking the boat.

My advice? I told her that she seemed to be a very ambitious and creative person. But no matter how hard she tried, her company and her managers were never going to change. It had taken them their entire lives to develop their personalities and surround themselves with other people with the same worldview. The best that she could do is to go to work for a younger, more dynamic company that would appreciate the energy and ideas that she wanted to bring to the work. She thanked me and walked away.

A year later, when I was speaking in the same city, she came up to me and reintroduced herself. She was beaming and happy. She had followed my advice. She found a three-year-old company that had been started by younger people, and she went to work with them at an entry-level job. Within a few months she had been promoted, and then promoted again, and promoted once more. Her income was up by 40 percent from what she was earning at the old job. Most of all, she told me that she was excited and happy about her work and looked forward to every new day.

The Right People in the Right Seats

The point is that you should never try to put a round peg into a square hole. Even if a person has the talents, abilities, and experience that you need and want, it is very important that the person be compatible with the culture of your company. If their personality and temperament is different from that of the key decision makers in your company, they will not work out over time, and you will simply have to go through the time and trouble of replacing them. Think it through in advance.

Once you have given considerable thought to the person you are looking for, and discussed it with others, and written out your thoughts on paper, it is now time to write out the job description in detail. Exactly what do you want the person to do?

Preparing the Job Description

List the exact output responsibilities of the job. List the education, skills, and experience that would be required of the ideal candidate. Describe the ideal personality or temperament that the new person would need to have to fit in well with you and the other people in your company.

Make a list of all the qualities and characteristics that the ideal person would have. This list may stretch to twenty or thirty items. Then organize the list and divide 100 points among the ingredients that the ideal candidate would possess, based on priorities.

What is the most important quality you are looking for? Usually it is a track record of previous success in getting results at the most important part of the job for which you are hiring this person. This item may be assigned 10 or 20 points, maybe even 50!

What is the second most important ingredient that you are looking for? What is the third? And so on. Keep working and reworking your list, dividing up the 100 points until you have what is basically an upside-down pyramid. You will find that 20 percent of the ingredients that you have identified as important for the job will take up more than 80 of the 100 points in describing the ideal person. Your list will also clearly fall into "musts" and "wants."

Separate Musts from Wants

There are certain things that you absolutely, positively must have in the ideal candidate. There are other things that would be nice to have, but they are not essential. For example, when I write up a description of the ideal person for a job, I always include, "Lives reasonably close to the office."

However, this requirement only gets one or two points when I compare it against skills, ability, and previous experience. This is a "want" that would be nice to have, but it is not an essential ingredient. Today, I have excellent staff members who live thirty and forty miles from the office.

At this stage, stop the clock and circulate your list and

your point-distribution scheme to the other members of your team. Invite them to comment on your description, and add in their own opinions. You'll be amazed at the valuable insights that your team members can give you.

Now you are ready to write an advertisement to attract the ideal person. This exercise crystallizes your best thinking. You can start off with a statement such as, "We are seeking a person with a proven track record in achieving the following results . . . ," and then you list the specific output responsibilities of the job. You can then list some of the desired personality attributes, such as "friendly, creative, good team player." Once more, you should circulate this advertisement/job description before you post it. You will always find ways to make it even better and more effective in attracting the right person.

Cast a Wide Net

Once you have a clear written description of the person you want, you should cast a wide net. Put out the word. Start with the Internet and post the description on Monster.com, CareerBuilder.com, and Craigslist. Invite prospective candidates to send their resumes by e-mail so that you can evaluate them and respond to them.

Some companies use another technique in addition to circulating the job description. They make every attempt to hire *internally*. They post the job description or tell as many people in the company as possible that they are looking for a person who fulfills these requirements.

One company offers a $1,500 bonus for each new person brought into the company by a current employee. It pays the bonus in three parts: $500 when the new person is hired, $500 after six months, and $500 at the end of one year.

Since each person in your company knows an average of

300 people by their first names, when you financially incentivize your staff to be on the lookout for people to join your company, you will be casting your net over hundreds and potentially thousands of candidates.

The best news is that your staff members have an insider's viewpoint on the very best kind of people to recommend for employment in your company. They don't want to make a mistake and be embarrassed by referring a person who doesn't work out. They will therefore be very discriminating about who they send to you to interview as a prospective employee.

Some companies do almost all of their hiring through internal referrals. You can also use newspapers, magazines, executive and personnel recruiters, and other media. It is a good idea to tell your vendors and suppliers that you are seeking a particular type of person and, if they come across the right candidate in the course of their work, that they should send them to you to interview.

Contact Community Colleges

An often-overlooked source of candidates is your local community college. Community college attendees range in age from 28 to 40 years old, on average. The number one reason that adults attend community college is to acquire skills that will make them more marketable and earn them bigger paychecks in the future. That's a good indication that the people who register and take these courses are usually ambitious, determined, and disciplined. They are exactly the kind of people you are seeking for your company.

Contact the community college, or colleges, within twenty-five miles of your location. Tell them that you are looking for one or more candidates to fill one or more specific job descriptions. E-mail them the job descriptions so that they have them in writing. If it is convenient, you might drop in and visit the community college and meet with the people in charge of job placement. These people are very eager to demonstrate that students taking courses at their college get better jobs soon after graduating. They will be wide open to cooperating with you.

The basic rule in hiring is that the greater the quantity of good candidates that you have, the better the quality of the candidates you finally select will be. The more people that you can attract to apply for a particular job or position, the better choice you will have in the end.

Sorting Job Applications

Now that you have put out the word that you are looking for a particular type of person, the next step is to handle the applications when they come in. It is not uncommon to receive dozens, even hundreds, of applications for a job when you post it online. You must learn how to winnow and sort through these applications quickly before you take any action.

You should only follow up on job applications that contain a direct response to you, referring to the job that you are offering. There should be something at the beginning of the response that is personalized and refers to your company or to the specific job or results that you are advertising for. Attached to that introduction should be a resume that tells you why this person is a good choice for the job you are advertising.

Screen Candidates by Phone

When you have sorted out the applications and reduced them to a manageable number, you e-mail the candidates and encourage them to phone you at a specific time for a telephone interview. You can sort out 80 percent to 90 percent of candidates on the telephone, without ever taking the time to meet with them personally. When they call, ask them questions that specifically relate to your advertisement and job description. Ask them why they feel that they can do this job. What experience do they have? What results have they achieved of a similar nature in the past? How many years of experience do they have?

Especially, ask them if they have visited your website. Then, ask them open-ended questions such as, What is your impression of our business? What would you say are the main products and services that we offer? In what area do you feel you would fit in best in our business? It is amazing the number of candidates who will call and apply for a job without ever visiting your website and studying it in any detail. This is a fast, easy way of qualifying candidates. If they have *not* visited your website, end the conversation, thank them for calling, and tell them that this job would not be the right job for them.

The Ideal Candidate Worth Meeting

What you are looking for are people who have read and studied the advertisement carefully. They have made some notes and thought about how they might qualify for the job. They have visited your website and explored it thoroughly, gaining an understanding of the size, nature, and structure of your business and your products and services. When you speak to them, they are knowledgeable, interested, and interesting. These are all good signs.

In an average job market, you may have to go through ten or twenty candidates to get one person worth meeting with. This is where the rubber meets the road. It is during the interviewing process, and afterward, that you increase or decrease your ability to hire the right person for you, and for the company.

The Law of Three in Hiring

The Law of Three is a powerful technique that you can use to increase the quality of your hires to as much as a 90 percent success rate. This principle forces you to slow down the hiring process and to make more accurate decisions. There are four applications of this law.

Interview Three Candidates

The first practice of the Law of Three is that you always interview at least three candidates for a job before you make a decision. No matter how good an impression a person makes at the first meeting, never make a job offer. Over time, managers find that the best that some people will ever look in their lives is at the first job interview. From that point onward, they often go downhill, and sometimes quite rapidly.

When you interview three different candidates, you get three different perspectives on the kind of people who are available. One person may look good to you, the second person may look average, and the third person may be an excellent choice. But in all cases, no matter how much you like the candidate, you put off the decision until a later time.

Interview Three Times

The second application of the Law of Three is that you interview the person that you like at least three times. Many companies interview a candidate, even for a secretarial position, as many as ten or twenty times. They know that by taking a long time in the selection process, they will get top people who will stay with the company for many years.

When you bring people back to interview them for the second time, their guard will be down considerably. You will observe things you missed completely the first time. When you interview the candidate the third time, if you do, you will often be amazed to think that you were considering hiring this person. By the third time that you meet with someone, you can see glaring discrepancies and weaknesses that you were not aware of earlier.

Select Three Different Meeting Places

The third application of the Law of Three is to interview the person in three different settings. People are subject to what is called the "chameleon effect." They change their personalities when you move them around, just as a chameleon changes its colors when you move it from place to place. A person who is professional, relaxed, and poised in your office may demonstrate a different personality when you take him across the street for a cup of coffee.

Your first meeting can be in your office, the second meeting can be in a staff room or another office down the hall, and your third meeting can be outside the office, at a venue for coffee or lunch. Many companies insist on taking the candidate and his or her spouse out for dinner before they make a hiring decision. As you move people around, they will demonstrate different facets of their personalities, sometimes admirable and sometimes not. The slower you go, the better decision you will make.

Have Three Different People Interview the Candidate

The next application of the Law of Three is to have the candidate interviewed by three other people. This is one of the most helpful rules I have ever learned as a manager. When I was a younger manager, and then a business owner, I would meet and hire people in a single meeting. As a result, there was a revolving door in my business. People were coming and going in as little as a day or two. This constant turnover created chaos, demoralization, confusion, and ended up costing an enormous amount of money over time.

When I began practicing the Law of Three, and slowing down the hiring process, the quality of my hires went up dramatically. But it was the fourth application of the principle that really helped. Now, once I have interviewed someone and am positively disposed toward hiring that person, I invite the person to go around the office and meet different people. I introduce all potential new hires to a person who will be a coworker if they are hired. After they have had a chat or cup of coffee together, sometimes lunch, that person will introduce them to the next coworker, and on down the line. Each of these conversations will be casual, one-on-one, peer-to-peer, completely nonthreatening, and relaxed.

After the candidate leaves, we assemble our team and take a vote. This vote is all or nothing. Our rule is that there must be a 100 percent consensus on hiring this person. Everyone must agree that this is the kind of person that they want to join our team. If even one of our valued team members disagrees, and their reason for disagreement cannot be dealt with satisfactorily, the candidate is disqualified from the running.

Getting the Team Involved

The advantages of involving the team are many. First, when your team members are involved in the interviewing and hiring process, they are much more engaged with the company than they would be if the new hire was just dropped in among them, like a fox among the chickens.

Second, when people have the opportunity to talk with and evaluate a potential teammate, and they vote to bring that person into the company, they will be much more committed to helping that person succeed from the very first day. They will take a personal interest in the career of that person.

They will feel that they had a substantial voice in hiring that person in the first place, and they will do everything to ensure that this person is successful.

From the first day, the new hires likewise find themselves surrounded by new friends. The members of your team will introduce themselves, offer to help in any way, have coffee with them, take them out for lunch, and even go for a drink after work. The new hires become an accepted part of the group immediately because the group was personally involved in bringing them on board.

The SWAN Formula

There are four things to look for in interviewing and hiring people. They should be *smart*, *work hard*, be *ambitious*, and be *nice*. This is often called the SWAN formula, after John Swan, the executive recruiter.

Look for Smart People

Intelligence is an excellent predictor of good performance. In terms of statistical variables, one study showed that intelligence among candidates had a 72 percent accuracy rate in predicting the success of a person in a new job. The smarter candidates were, the more likely it was that they would be ideal for the job.

One part of intelligence is educational background. The more education people have completed, the more likely they are to be more intelligent. Another indication is the amount of reading and self-development they do. The more well-read individuals are, and the more they listen to audio programs and take additional courses on their own, the more intelligent and productive they are likely to be.

A manager I knew developed an effective way of sorting out poor candidates from good ones. At the initial interview, his first question was, "Tell me about some of the books, audio programs, and seminars that you have read, listened to, or taken for your own personal and professional development."

Then he would just wait silently. If the candidate could not come up with any answers to that question, he would get up, thank the person for coming in, lead him to the door, and tell him that this was not the right job for him. What he had found, in years of hard experience, was that a person who was not interested in continuous learning was not a person who would be successful in the long term in his business.

You know the old saying, "If you're not getting better, you're getting worse." People who are not reading and upgrading their skills are actually sliding backward in a fast-moving, high-tech world. Look for people who are smart, and who are getting smarter.

Perhaps the best indication of intelligence is whether the person shows curiosity. Intelligent people ask a lot of questions. Average people just sit there and try to tell you what you want to hear. Especially, intelligent people want to know a lot about the business, the products and services, the potential future of the business, the industry, and how they might develop themselves if they come to work for this company. They ask a lot of questions about you as well. They are interested and engaged.

Look for Hard Workers

Look for people who will be hard workers. The 80/20 rule applies to work. Eighty percent of people working today are *lazy*. They are lazy, lazier, or extremely lazy. But they are basically lazy in that they are continually looking for ways to cut corners and do less work. They start at the last minute and they quit at the first minute. They waste an enormous amount of time chatting with coworkers and doing personal business that has nothing whatsoever to do with the job for which they have been hired.

People who work hard become what one author called "outperformers." They are the horses that pull the wagon, the locomotives that pull the train. It is the outperformers that do 80 percent of the work and are responsible for 80 percent of your success. Your job is to hire as many of them as possible.

A good question you can ask to determine how hard they work is this: "Sometimes we have to work evenings and weekends to get the job completed on schedule. How would you feel about that?" This question will usually smoke out a lazy person right away. They will start to hem and haw about how important their personal life and their weekends are to them. They will offer to work hard during the day but they don't like the idea of having to work extra hours. Just listen quietly and make a note to yourself. A person who will not work overtime will not work very hard during regular hours, either.

The correct answer to this question is simple. "Whatever it takes!"

A candidate who is a hard worker will do whatever it takes to do the job well, no matter how many hours it takes, no matter how many evenings and weekends are required. But people can fool you, so when checking references, be sure that you ask, "On a scale of one to ten, how hard a worker would you say this person is?"

Want Someone Who Wants to Get Ahead

The best candidates are *ambitious*. They want to get ahead in life. In fact, one of the most powerful motivators for top performance is the idea of moving upward and onward as a result of doing the job in an excellent fashion.

In today's job market, you may interview a candidate who has had several job changes in the last few years. This can be *bad* if the candidate was fired or laid off for poor performance. This can be *good* if the candidate is ambitious and has deliberately changed jobs seeking opportunities to do more and earn more.

A good question to ask is: "Where do you see yourself in the next three to five years?"

Many people will say, "I want your job."

The best answer is when people tell you that they want an opportunity to do an excellent job, to be promoted as a result, and to be paid more based on their performance. They will even ask what they have to do in order to be paid more money as soon as possible. This is the kind of person you can point in the right direction, who will work day and night to take advantage of the opportunity.

Hire Nice People

The fourth quality you are looking for is someone who is *nice*. Be perfectly selfish. Only hire people you personally like and enjoy. Never hire people with difficult personalities because of their technical skills or because you think that other people might like them or tolerate them.

The Articulate Incompetent

In looking for nice people, beware of "articulate incompetents." These people are everywhere today, going from job interview to job interview, getting jobs, and disrupting the workplace. They are a manager's worst nightmare.

Every manager eventually meets, and even hires, one or more of them. These people have only one skill: the ability to interview well for a job. They are pleasant, friendly, charming, have a good sense of humor, ask you a lot of questions about yourself, and seem to be fascinated with you and your personal history. You warm up to them almost immediately. But interviewing well is their *only* skill.

Once you hire an articulate incompetent, you will find that the person never produces anything of value. These individuals are incredibly artful with excuses and dodges. They always have a reason why the job has not been done. They are always talking about the great job that they are just about to do. They warm up to and make friends with everybody, and often become quite popular, at least in the short term. But they never seem to do anything of value.

Even worse, in three to six months, articulate incompetents will come to you with a list of excuses and reasons why they haven't quite gotten the job done yet, but they will want a large increase in pay. They will try to convince you that, if only they were earning enough to solve their financial problems, they would be doing a much better job.

In my experience, it usually takes about six months to spot an articulate incompetent. During that time you are shaking your head, and sometimes tearing out your hair, because you cannot quite figure out what is happening. It is only when you realize that you have been hoodwinked by a professional job interviewer that you stop the clock, call a time-out, and get rid of the person. If you are having this experience today, or if you have had this experience in the past, don't feel bad about it. It is an almost inevitable rite of passage in becoming a manager.

Achievement History

When you interview candidates, look for achievement history and their past performance. What specifically have they done in the past to demonstrate that they can get the results that you are hiring them to achieve in the future? Remember, people evaluate themselves based on what they think they can do in the future. But you must only evaluate people based on what they have done in the past. Past performance is the only predictor of future performance.

One of the best qualities that I have found in a good candidate is a "sense of urgency." The candidate wants the job, wants it badly, and wants to start as soon as possible. Yet this can be a telltale giveaway, too. People will often interview enthusiastically and well for a job, but when you ask them when they can start, they start to talk about needing to give their boss several weeks notice, or wanting to take a vacation before they start a new job. Whenever you hear these stories, alarm bells should go off.

If this is the right candidate for you and your company, the person will be eager to start the job as soon as possible. The right candidates will be thinking about how they can get out of their current position, and even offer to work part-time in the evenings and weekends to get up to speed for when they are ready to work full-time. Anyone who wants to take some time to think about it, delay, or take a vacation should be eliminated from consideration immediately.

Don't Start Selling Yet

One more point with regard to interviewing: Don't start *selling* until you are ready to *buy*. Don't launch into a wonderful description of the joys of the job and the wonders of the company before you have even reached the point where you are convinced you want to hire this person in the first place.

Many managers make the mistake of turning the job interview into a sales pitch. They talk on and on about the wonderful people and glorious future for people working there.

They try to impress the candidate with what a great company it is.

There is a correct time for explaining the company's best qualities and what a good career decision it would be to come and work for this company. But it comes later in the interview. It comes after you begin to get a feeling that this may be the right candidate for you, once the person indicates she's really curious to know more about the future of the company. Be patient. Take your time. Don't start selling until you have decided to buy.

Checking Resumes Carefully

Once you have decided that you like a candidate, or even before, you should check the references that accompany the individual's CV. About 60 percent of resumes are falsified in some way. Educational credentials are exaggerated. Accomplishments are overstated. The level of authority and responsibility attained is overblown. The previous salary is puffed up. No matter how much you like the person, never accept anything on faith.

A good idea is to tell the candidate, "We are going to do a complete background check on the information provided in your resume. Is there anything else that we should know before we begin our research?"

This simple question often brings skeletons out of the closet, some of which you will be able to deal with and some of which will be deal breakers. Making this statement can also save you a lot of time and trouble in checking resumes or in failing to uncover fatal flaws.

Expect Cautious Responses

When you follow up with a referral listed on a resume, remember that most employers are gun-shy of being sued for making any kind of negative statement about a past employee. They will be careful and guarded. They will often be instructed to give you nothing more than the dates of employment and the position the employee had.

Checking resumes is something that you need to do *personally,* if the person is going to work for you directly. It is not an activity that you can delegate to a secretary or another subordinate. You need to be able to speak directly to a person in your position in another company, and to listen to both what is said and what isn't said in the conversation.

Ask for Help

When you get the referral on the phone, introduce yourself, then tell the person that you are a manager of your company and that you are talking to this particular individual about coming to work for you. Say these words: "I need your help."

Tell the person about the job that you are hiring the candidate to do. Ask how well he thinks that the candidate might perform in this job. Speak as little as possible and listen carefully.

The two questions that you can ask, both of which will often give you valuable insights, are these:

1. "Would you hire this person back again today?" Legally, people can answer this question honestly and directly without any fear of being sued. If they say that they would not hire the candidate back, you ask, "May I ask why not?" You may or may not get an answer, but always ask.

2. "Is there anything else I should know about this person?" Ask this question just before you hang up. Sometimes, the answer to this question will give you vital information that will allow you to make a much better hiring decision.

Make the Decision Slowly

Once you have done your interviewing and your homework and are about to make the hiring decision, stop for a while longer and take some time to think about it in greater depth. Make your decision slowly.

One manager I worked with developed a reputation over the years of hiring truly excellent people who went on to be promoted and become valuable parts of the company. His secret was simple. "No matter how much I like a person, I always wait for thirty days before I make the hiring decision."

At the very least, sleep on the decision before you make it. If possible, think about it over the weekend. To buy time for myself, I often encourage the candidate to think about it as well. "Take a couple of days to think about it, and if you still really want this job, call me back on Monday afternoon around three."

Listen to Your Intuition

One of the best things you can do is to follow your intuition. Trust your "inner voice." Tune in to your instincts. If you listen to your inner voice, you'll probably never make another mistake. If for any reason you are unsure or uncomfortable with the idea of hiring a person, you should not hire him at all. Sooner or later you will find that this inner sense or "gut feeling" was correct. Never go against it.

The Twenty-Year Method

If you still need help making a decision, try the twenty-year method. Imagine that you will be coming to work and seeing this person each day for the next twenty years. Imagine that this person is going to be a permanent part of your work life, for the rest of your career. How would you feel about that? When you ask yourself this question, you may find that you do not like the idea of having to work with this person for the next two decades. This method might just give you an insight into the right decision to make.

You can also use the "family member method." How would you feel about bringing this person home to have dinner with your family on Sunday night? Would you be comfortable having this person around your family dinner table? Would you be happy having your son or daughter work under this person? If not, why not?

The rule is that the longer you take to decide, the better decision you will make. Your ability to hire the right person for your team is one of the most important skills you ever develop as a manager or business owner. And fortunately, you can get better and better at hiring good people by going a little bit slower, following the ideas in this chapter, and by regularly reviewing your hiring decisions to see how they turned out.

Action Exercises

1. Identify the best people who have ever worked for you. What did they have in common?

2. Think about the worst people who have ever worked for you. What did they have in common?

3. Get your team's opinion. What is the best advantage you can gain by having your team members involved in the hiring decisions?

4. Describe (on paper) the most important things you need to look for in hiring anyone.

5. Evaluate the candidate's previous achievements as the best predictors of future performance.

6. Create a list of all the qualities and characteristics you want in the ideal candidate for a particular job. Which is most important?

7. Reflect on this question: Is there anyone working for you today who, knowing what you now know, you wouldn't hire back again today?

CHAPTER EIGHT

Results Are Everything

"If you go to work on your goals, your goals will go
to work on you. If you go to work on your plan,
your plan will go to work on you. Whatever good
things we build, end up building us."

—JIM ROHN

In this book, you have learned how to motivate your employees. You have learned how to build up their self-esteem, self-ideal, and self-image, drive away their fears, and make them feel like winners. However, as a manager and a leader, you are not doing all of this to make people feel good about themselves. Your goal—your only ultimate goal—is to get results.

Results are everything.

Results are the beginning, middle, and end of all organizations. You get results by combining the complementary talents and abilities of several people to achieve goals that would not be possible for a single person working alone. It doesn't matter how much people like themselves or feel important if the results don't follow.

Remember, you are not a cheerleader; you are not a life coach. You are a manager and a leader. Your responsibility is to get results.

It Starts with You

What results are expected of you? Of all the results that are expected of you, what is the most important result? If you could only achieve one result in an excellent fashion, what would that one result be? What is the one result that you must achieve to ensure the success of your business or department?

Results are specific, measurable, and time-bounded. They are simple and clear, and can be explained to a child. Einstein once said, "If you cannot explain what you are attempting to accomplish to a six-year-old child, then you are probably not clear about it yourself."

Think on paper. Make a list of all the results that are expected of you in your position. Organize them by priority. Select the one result that, if you achieved it, would have a greater impact on your career and your success than any other single result.

Making It Measurable

How will you know that you have achieved this result? If the result is large or longer term, what are the interim results or measures that you have to accomplish, the steps on the staircase, to achieve the ultimate result? The very process of thinking through the steps that you need to follow to achieve your goal greatly simplifies and accelerates the process of accomplishment. As Henry Ford said, "Any goal can be achieved if you break it down into enough small steps."

Strive for excellence. Set BHAGs (big hairy audacious goals) for yourself and for your team. "Dream big dreams; only big dreams have the power to move men's souls."

Even if you are starting or operating a small business, or are in charge of part of the business, imagine what you would have to do to achieve world-class status and dominate your market.

When I speak to entrepreneurs and would-be business owners, they continually ask me what they need to do to be successful. I explain to them repeatedly that results are everything. You must maintain a single-minded focus on getting the most important results for which you are responsible.

The Promises You Make

The only question that a prospective customer has for whatever you sell is, "Does it work?" Does your product or service actually deliver the results or benefits that you say it will, repeatedly and consistently, over and over again? Philip Crosby's definition of quality is that "your product or service does what you say it will do when you sell it and continues to do it." Your "quality rating" is the percentage of times that you deliver on this promise.

My favorite definition of *branding* is that your brand is composed of two things: the promises you make, and the promises you keep. Your *personal* brand, which is the way people think and talk about you, and is the critical determinant of your success and rewards, is largely made up of the promises you make, in terms of the results that you agree to achieve, and the promises you keep, which are those results that you consistently deliver.

Clarity is essential and consistency is the key. If you could achieve a single result consistently, over and over without fail, what one result would help you and your business the most? What one result would have the greatest positive impact on your business? Whatever it is, write it down, make a plan, and focus on achieving that result every single day.

The Law of Three

In working with thousands of businesspeople, I have discovered that there is a Law of Three in business management. In the bigger picture, there are only three things that your company does that account for 90 percent of the value, the sales, revenues, income, profitability, and growth of your business. These three results that you get for your customers change as the economy, markets, and customer preferences change, but there are usually only three. For example, these three may be (1) new product or service creation; (2) aggressive and effective marketing; and (3) great customer service. In times of turbulence, when you experience resistance or setbacks in the market, it is important that you take a time-out and identify those three critical results that customers care about the most, and will pay the most to enjoy, in competition with other businesses that are pursuing the same customer dollar.

In addition, there seems to be one major result that you must achieve, and two complementary results that are essential to achieving the main result. What are they for *your* business? For example, the key result could be sales volume, and the complementary results could be effective marketing, to attract qualified prospects, and effective selling, to convert these prospects into customers.

Your Personal Big Three

In your personal work, the Law of Three applies as well. It says that there are only three things that you do that constitute 90 percent of the contribution you make to your business. What are they?

According to this law, then, aside from the three most important tasks or results you achieve, everything else—or the majority of your activities—contribute 10 percent, or little or nothing at all, in terms of actual results. The sad thing is that most people spend 90 percent of their time on the activities that contribute very little, and then they wonder why they are making so little progress.

Two Pitfalls to Avoid

There are two mental pitfalls that stand in the way of you and your people working on your highest value tasks and accomplishing the most important goals that you need to accomplish to satisfy the greatest number of customers. These pitfalls are (1) the comfort zone and (2) the path of least resistance.

■ *The Comfort Zone.* People fall into a comfort zone as naturally and as easily as they choose or mix their coffee the same way, every single time. Most of what you do—95 percent of it—is determined by your *habits*. There's a saying: "Good habits are hard to form but easy to live with; bad habits are easy to form but hard to live with."

Habits are good because they enable us to do routine tasks in an easy and automatic way without thinking very much about them. This type of habit frees up our minds to do more complex and demanding work that requires creativity and initiative, and that cannot be accomplished in a routine way, or simply by going through the motions.

Yet habits can be self-sabotaging when you get into a routine of doing things of little value at work rather than disciplining yourself to work on those few things that can really make a difference.

All change and improvement requires that you break out of the comfort zone of working on small, easy, enjoyable, and (unfortunately) irrelevant tasks and activities, and discipline yourself to work single-mindedly on only those top *three* activities that contribute the utmost value to yourself and your business. The comfort zone is like gravity. It is constantly pulling you down toward things that you have done in the past, even if those activities are no longer helpful or useful.

The reason that change of any kind, even positive change that everyone agrees is necessary, is so difficult is because people are locked into their comfort zones and naturally resist doing anything new or different.

■ *The Path of Least Resistance.* This second pitfall is the twin sister of the comfort zone; they go around together and support each other. The path of least resistance is perhaps the greatest of all enemies of personal and business success. It says that people tend to seek the fastest and easiest way to get what they want, right now, with little consideration of the long-term consequences of their acts. In other words, most people seek the most effortless way of performing any task or achieving any result.

This tendency is *helpful* when it leads to finding faster, better, cheaper, and more convenient ways to accomplish tasks, produce products and services, and satisfy customers. But it is *harmful* when it causes people to seek shortcuts, slack off, consume half of their time each day in idle chitchat with coworkers, surfing the Internet, taking long coffee breaks and lunches, or doing personal business and other activities that contribute absolutely nothing to the results they have been hired to accomplish.

The only way that you can avoid a pitfall, or escape from it, is to be aware of it. The comfort zone and the path of least resistance beckon you enticingly every minute of every day. You must consciously and continuously resist their blandishments and instead keep focused on doing those few things that make the greatest difference in your life and in your career.

Planning for Results

Here is a simple exercise: Make a list of all the results that are expected of you. Then ask yourself, "If I could only achieve *one result* on this list in an excellent fashion consistently, over and over again, which one result would make the greatest contribution to my business?"

Put a circle around that task or activity. Then ask the question again: "If I could only achieve *two* results on this list, which would be the second most important result that I could accomplish?" Put a circle around that.

Then, do this exercise one more time. What would be the *third* result on your list that could make the greatest contribution to yourself and your business?

In doing this exercise, you will be surprised to see how important these three results are, and how secondary or irrelevant are all the other little tasks and activities on your list.

The next part of this exercise is obvious. Make a second list of everything that you could do in the course of a day or a month to achieve the most important results expected of you. Write down all your tasks and activities, from Monday morning to Friday night, and throughout your days and weeks. Once your list is complete, review your list and ask this question: "If I could only complete *one task* on this list, which one task would have the greatest impact in achieving the most important result expected of me?"

Put a circle around that number on your list. Then ask yourself the question again: "If I could only accomplish two tasks on this list, which would be the *second task* that would help me the most to make the maximum contribution to myself and my business?"

Put a circle around this task and then ask the question one more time. What would be the third task?

The final part of this exercise is simple. Once you have determined the *three* most important results you can get, and the *three* most important activities that you can engage in to get your three most important results, select the *one* activity that is most important to getting your most important results and begin on it immediately. Then, discipline yourself to work single-mindedly on accomplishing that one task, even if it takes many hours and forces you to put everything else aside, until that task is accomplished.

The Key to Your Success

In decades of research into personal effectiveness, efficiency, and performance, I have found that this simple, three-part exercise is the key to all success, accomplishment, and achievement. It is the key to getting paid more and promoted faster. More than anything else, it is the key to achieving ever-higher levels of personal self-esteem, self-respect, and personal pride. I highly recommend that you do this exercise if you want to become the most valuable person you can possibly become.

When you are working on the most important thing that

you could be doing, you feel happier and better about your-self. Your brain releases endorphins, which give you a sense of elation and make you more creative and personable. You discover you have an endless flow of energy that actually moves you onto a higher plain of personal performance. The regular habit of starting and finishing your most important tasks unlocks your potential and enables you to step on the accelerator of your career.

Keeping Everyone Focused

Once you have performed this exercise for yourself, deter-mining the most important results that you have been tasked to accomplish, and determining the most important things you can do to achieve those results, your next step is to design and structure your company or department in such a way that everyone around you does the same thing. Help them to determine their three most important results, the three most important tasks they could complete to achieve those results, and the single most important task they could be working on at the moment to make the greatest possible contribution to your business.

You should always start your planning process, or your replanning process, by defining jobs in terms of results ex-pected. The reason is that sometimes one person can achieve several of the results on your list. You can then search for a person who has the blended skills and experience to accom-plish multiple tasks. This is important when you are starting and building a business and equally as important in times of budget cuts and constrained resources.

Matching Skills to Results Required

Once you have defined the results required to accomplish the overall results for which you are responsible, you then make a list of the specific skills that one or more of your employees will have to have to achieve those results. Again, depending upon your budget and your circumstances, your very best course of action might be to look for a person with multiple skills who can accomplish multiple results. It is often a better idea to be willing to pay more for such a person than to think of hiring two or more people to do the job.

Here's another exercise you can try: To clearly define the results that you require, try writing them down on sticky notes and laying them out on a large sheet of paper or whiteboard in front of you. Sometimes you can make them into headers, running across the top of the page. These are the results expected. Next, to define the skills necessary to accomplish those results, you can use smaller sticky notes and list the skills in a vertical column under the header listing the result.

With this visual picture of the results you need and the skills that will be required to achieve those results, you can then organize those skills in order of priority. Which is more important? Which is less important? Which is essential? Which is helpful but not essential?

By creating a visual picture of the results desired and the skills necessary to achieve them, you then have the opportunity to move the sticky notes around until you have a clear definition of a job that needs to be done and the proven skills that a person must have to do that job in an excellent fashion.

Determining Who Is Going to Do What

You have to decide whether one or more of the jobs that need to be done can be combined and done by a single person. Always think in terms of expanding the responsibilities of a particular position rather than expanding the size of your workforce.

When you start a new business or department, you always start off by defining the work that has to be done before you determine exactly who is going to do the work. For example, when two or more partners start a business, or when you start a business and you already have one or more employees, you begin by defining all the functions that must be performed. You then determine, based on experience and ability, which person is best qualified to perform those functions.

When William Hewlett and David Packard formed Hewlett-Packard Company in Palo Alto, California, in 1948, they were both engineers with extensive backgrounds. But they decided from the beginning that Hewlett would focus on developing products, like their first oscilloscope, and Packard would focus on marketing those products. Hewlett on the inside; Packard on the outside. This division of responsibilities, determined at the founding of the company, has enabled Hewlett-Packard to grow to be a world leader with 120,000 employees. The company (now known only as HP) still employs the same principles of defining jobs in terms of output responsibilities required, and then filling those jobs with the person most capable of achieving those results.

The Big Question

As you build your business, one of the most important questions that each person in the business can ask is, "Why am I on the payroll?" What exactly have you been hired to accomplish? Of all the things that you are expected to do, what are the most important?

You should teach the Law of Three and help all of the people working for the business to analyze their work and determine the three most important things they do, day in and day out, that make their most valuable contribution to the business. Have employees make a list of everything they do, from the beginning of the month to the end, and then organize that list by priority, based on their personal evaluation. Have each staff member bring the list to you so that you can both discuss the employee's conclusions and comment on his evaluation of priorities and results expected.

It is absolutely amazing how many managers are not really clear about *why* each specific person is on the payroll. They have a general knowledge of the overall job description of the individual, but they are not completely clear on the big question: Why?

Keeping Your Job

Often, when I speak to groups of managers, I introduce them to a game. The game is called "Keep Your Job." I tell them that once I explain the rules of the game they can decide if they would like to play.

Here are the rules: First, I ask the managers to make a list of all of the people who report to them. Then, the managers would make a list of the three most important things that each person on their list has been hired to accomplish, their highest priority tasks, in order of importance.

Once the people have been identified, and their three most important tasks have been listed next to each name, the next part of the game is simple. I tell them that they have to sit here and wait while I go and speak to each of their employees. I will ask the employees to write down why they feel they are on the payroll and the three most important tasks that they have been hired to accomplish. If the answers of each of the staff members are the same as the answers that the manager has written, those managers get to "keep their job."

Then I ask, "How many people here would like to play?"

In several years of introducing this game, and the rules of the game, I have never had a manager raise his hand to participate.

Perhaps the most powerful of all motivations, as I repeat over and over, is for individuals to be absolutely clear about exactly what is expected of them, and in what order of priority. The kindest and most helpful thing that you can do to immediately increase productivity, performance, and morale is to take the time to sit down with your staff members, one by one, and review their output responsibilities, helping them to set clear priorities on what is more valuable and what is less valuable.

Why You Must Clarify Continually

In my company, and in many companies that I have worked with, especially in times of rapid change and turbulence, when job descriptions become obsolete almost as soon as the ink is dry on them, we have a regular "Why am I on the payroll?" day.

Here is how it works. Employees are requested to write up their own job description. On this job description, they write down their primary responsibilities first. These primary responsibilities, usually three to five, are the most important things that they have been tasked to accomplish. These are the real reasons they are on the payroll. These are the most important contributions they can make to the company.

The second category is called "secondary responsibilities." On this list, employees write down all of the smaller things that they do, support activities and complementary activities that are not a main part of their jobs, but are tasks and responsibilities that they fulfill whenever they are required or necessary.

It's as Simple as Answering the Phone

Sometimes, a secondary responsibility can be something as simple as answering the telephone. For example, several times when I was traveling, I called my office. After the phone rang several times, I would be transferred to the company voice mail system and told to "leave a message."

Since our business, like most businesses, is highly dependent on customers calling in and placing orders, this failure to be able to get through to my own company when I phoned was a source of great concern to me. When I got back from my trip, I called a staff meeting and explained my experience. I told them that if the owner of the company cannot get his phone calls answered when he phones during the working day, the same thing must be happening repeatedly to customers who are calling to place orders. This situation is costing us sales and a lot of money (not to mention damaging our reputation). What on earth was going on?

Everyone Is Innocent

After a lot of glancing around the room, mumbling, and double-talking, we figured out what the problem was: It turned out that everyone thought they were doing their jobs exactly as they had been instructed to. No one felt responsible for this problem because no one had been told that one of the job's secondary responsibilities was to answer the telephone when it wasn't answered immediately by the receptionist or by someone in customer service.

In my experience, when there is a problem like this, based on poor instruction by the manager or misunderstandings by the staff, no one is really at fault. No one is guilty. No one is to be blamed or punished. The secondary responsibility for answering the phone in this case was something that had fallen through the cracks and no one was aware of it. It was merely a problem that needed to be solved, and solved quite quickly.

We immediately agreed that the telephones would be answered in a specific sequence. When the phone rang the first time, the receptionist would answer and then transfer the call to the proper person. If the receptionist was away or tied up on another call and the phone rang twice, someone else was specifically tasked to answer the phone at that time. If the phone rang three times, indicating that the first two people were tied up with callers, someone else was specifically tasked to answer the phone at that time. In addition, if people were going to be away from their desks or otherwise unable to answer the phone when it rang, they would be responsible for alerting others to the fact that answering the phone was now their secondary responsibility. Within a few hours, the problem was solved and did not arise again.

Everyone Understands Everyone's Job

Once all employees have written out their job descriptions, with primary responsibilities listed on the top half of the page and secondary responsibilities listed on the bottom half of the page, they are requested to make copies for everyone on the team. We then get together in a meeting and people hand out their job descriptions to each other.

We then review the job descriptions as a group. One individual describes her job, the order of priority, exactly what she does to achieve that result, and any problems or difficulties she is having. Each member of the team is encouraged to ask questions or comment on that person's job description. At the end of the discussion, everyone is crystal clear about what that person is expected to do, and in what order of priority.

We then go on to the second person. Once that person

has described his job and it has been thoroughly discussed and evaluated by the team, we go on to the third person, and so on. At the end of the meeting, everyone is clear about what everyone else is doing, in what order of priority, and how their jobs are to be measured.

Open Inquiry Eliminates Confusion and Contradiction

When you conduct this exercise for the first time, you will be amazed at the confusion, contradiction, and lack of clarity that people have about what other people are doing. Some people will be of the impression that what is someone else's area of primary responsibility is their area of primary responsibility. Others will learn that what they thought was their area of primary responsibility is not their job at all. It belongs to someone else. People will find that an area of secondary responsibility is actually the most important reason that they are on the payroll.

In the course of the discussion, all of these inconsistencies are resolved and dealt with in a spirit of open inquiry. At the end of the meeting, all employees have far greater clarity on where they stand, the importance of their job, and, most of all, what everyone else is doing—and their order of priority as well.

Whenever you find that, because of continuous change in job descriptions and responsibilities, certain tasks begin to fall between the cracks and either don't get done at all or get done in a poor fashion, you should call a "why am I on the payroll" meeting. The results of these meetings will save you a fortune in lost time and wasted effort, quite apart from the cost of lost sales, lost customers, and lost business.

Five Keys to Peak Performance

There are five keys to building a peak performance work environment. These five factors have been identified by exhaustive research and experience in large and small companies over the years. They are simple and easy to apply, and should be part of your vision for your ideal business or motivational environment.

1. *Shared Goals and Objectives.* Each person needs to know exactly why the company or department exists, what it is trying to accomplish, its most important goals and objectives, and its reason for existence.

The more opportunity that people have to discuss, debate, and disagree about the goals and objectives of the business, the greater clarity they have about why it is they are on the payroll, and the greater commitment they have to working well with others to accomplish the goals and achieve the desired results.

2. *Shared Values.* Everyone on the team should be clear about the basic principles or values that determine how team members interact and relate with each other. These values always exist, at one level or another, either explicitly stated or merely assumed. But they need to be clear to everyone.

When you write out these values and virtues, and discuss what they are and what they mean, and especially how they will be enacted in day-to-day work, you dramatically increase the level of commitment to these values and the likelihood that they will be followed by everyone. Here is an exercise that you can do in values clarification:

■ Have staff members bring to the meeting a list of the five most important values that they feel should govern the interactions and relationships among other team members. Have people read aloud their values and have someone write them down on a flip chart or a whiteboard. Right away, you will discover that many of these values are repeated—values such as integrity, quality, excellence, respect for individuals, responsibility, and so on.

■ Select three to five values. As you write down the values, put a mark next to each value that is repeated. At the end of the exercise, three to five values will clearly be more popular than any of the other values. You then have people write down, from the three to five values that get the highest scores, the three values that they consider to be the most relevant and important. One person then takes these ballots or votes with the list of three values from each person and quickly summarizes the result to see which values have "won" the popularity contest. These values are then written out on the whiteboard for everyone to see.

■ Discuss how these values will be practiced in the day-to-day work. You discuss the importance of values such as honesty, respect for each other, acceptance of responsibility, quality work, punctuality, and so on.

■ Create a consensus. Once everyone has had a chance to contribute their ideas of what values are most helpful, and has had an opportunity to vote, and the votes have been crystallized into the most popular values, a consensus will form around these values. When each person has an opportunity to discuss what these values actually mean in practice, you will create total engagement. From this moment on, everyone will be committed to practicing the values in everything they do. This acts as a tremendous motivator of performance and enables you to solve problems and make decisions far faster than if these values were unclear or undetermined.

3. *Shared Plans of Action.* This takes us back to the "Why am I on the payroll?" question. It is important, for maximum performance, that everyone knows what everyone else on the team is supposed to be doing, and in what order of priority,

and on what schedule. The greater clarity that people have with regard to the work that everyone around them is doing, the more positive and motivated everyone will be.

In addition, people will be far more cooperative and helpful with other team members if they know what the other team member is supposed to accomplish. They will recognize when one person is overwhelmed and step in to help. They will offer suggestions on how the job can be done faster and better. The more clarity that each person has about the work of each other person, the faster and more efficiently the job will be done, and with fewer mistakes.

4. *Leadership for the Team.* Your job as a manager, from this point on, is to help your team to fulfill their responsibilities. Rather than being an "orchestra director" or "sergeant major," your job is to be a "blocker." Your job is to make sure that people have the resources they need and to remove the obstacles that stand in their way from accomplishing their tasks in the very best way possible.

Your primary question as the manager is, "What can I do to help?"

Of course, you have your own part of the work to do, but your primary role as manager is to make sure that everyone else can do their job as quickly and as well as possible. By taking this role as a "helper," everyone sees you as a valued partner in the work. This builds commitment, dedication, and loyalty, and a desire for others to help you and to help everyone else to be more successful.

5. *Continuous Evaluation and Appraisal.* The very best teams are staffed with people who are committed to success, to doing the job well. If, for any reason, some people are not fulfilling their responsibilities or carrying their fair share of the load, excellent teams deal with such problems and disagreements with openness and honesty.

You should continually be asking the question, "How are we doing?" How is the business doing in terms of the people who use your services or consume the results that you produce? How are you doing in terms of how well the team is functioning together? Most of all, how can you improve? What should you be doing more of or less of to get better results? What should you start doing or stop doing to improve performance and effectiveness?

All of life, especially at work, is a series of "two steps forward and one step back." You are continually getting feedback and making course corrections. No process is ever perfect. Misunderstandings and mistakes are an inevitable and unavoidable part of the work process.

Thinking in Terms of Solutions

Perhaps one of the most important attitudes that you can instill in yourself and your team is a "solutions orientation." Encourage everyone to think continually in terms of the solutions to the inevitable problems and obstacles that will occur every single day. Instead of making excuses or looking for someone to blame, you should always look for the solution to the problems, to what can be done immediately to solve the problem and to move forward toward achieving the results expected.

When everyone is encouraged to think of solutions and the actions that they can take to implement those solutions, everyone's thinking becomes more positive, creative, and forward-directed. Instead of worrying about what went wrong and who could have done or not done something, everyone thinks about how to correct the situation and make more immediate progress. This automatically elicits a positive, creative, and optimistic worldview, creates peak performance teams, and makes people really happy about being part of this organization.

Creating Your Ideal Team

Your job, as the leader, is to take the time to think through the ideal structure of your team. Think through the exact results that must be accomplished overall, and the specific results that must be accomplished to achieve the major result.

Identify the talents and skills that people will need to achieve the results for which you, and they, are responsible. Hire people as much for their personality as their technical competence. When in doubt, always seek people who will fit in well with the team, who will get along with others and be popular in the work group.

A positive group of happy people, working together with clear goals and objectives, can accomplish extraordinary things, even against enormous competition in the marketplace. Your ability to design this ideal team, and then to work continuously to help this team to perform at their best, is perhaps the most valuable contribution you can make to your business.

Action Exercises

1. If your team was perfect and doing a great job at getting the most important results for which you are responsible, how would it be different from today?
2. What are the three most important results that you have been tasked to accomplish?
3. What are the three most important results that you are personally responsible for achieving?
4. What are the three most important tasks that you do that make the biggest difference to your business and to your own personal success?

5. Who are your most important people and what are the three most important things they do to get the most important results? Do they know? Would you like to play a round of "Keep Your Job"?

6. What one change should you make immediately that would help you to create a better and more productive team?

7. Organize a "Why am I on the payroll?" meeting as soon as possible. Help your employees to develop absolute clarity about their primary and secondary responsibilities.

CHAPTER NINE

Be the Best You Can Be

"If we did all the things we are capable of,
we would literally astonish ourselves."

—THOMAS EDISON

All the techniques and knowledge in the world won't motivate people who have no confidence in the skills and vision of
their leaders. Giving praise is a motivator—unless that praise
comes from a leader who does not have the respect of the
employee. A manager who is seen as a failure by his staff or
his workforce can never build the self-esteem of that workforce because whatever he says or does won't matter.

In this final chapter, I am going to focus on you, the
leader, and what you can do to become the best leader and
manager you can be. Get ready to learn the seventeen greatest management principles ever discovered. If you adhere to

these principles you can earn the respect and admiration of your employees and colleagues by becoming one of the most efficient, effective, productive, and admired people in your organization.

Management Is a Learnable Skill

Over the past thirty years, I have worked with more than 1,000 businesses, large and small, from entrepreneurial start-ups to Fortune 500 companies. In every case, I have been searching for the so-called "secrets of success" in management and the answer to the question: Why is it that some managers are more successful than others?

What I have learned is that management is a profession. It is both an art and a science. It is based on technique and methodology. There are certain things that you can do that will bring you extraordinary results as a manager in getting the job done, on time and on schedule.

And what anyone else has done, you can do as well. No one is better than you and no one is smarter than you. The reason that some managers are outperforming other managers is because they have learned what to do and what not to do. They have applied these key lessons, over and over again, until they have mastered them.

Being the best manager and leader you can be is the foundation of motivation. You become an effective motivator of others only after proving that you have integrity, intelligence, vision, creativity, persistence, and the continuous desire to improve yourself and grow your people.

Three Key Orientations

All successful managers have three key orientations. First, they are *result-oriented*. They are intensely focused on getting the job done and getting it done well. Second, they are *solu-*

tion-oriented. They are intensely focused on finding the solutions to the obstacles and difficulties that occur all day long, rather than making excuses or blaming other people. Third, all successful managers are intensely *action-oriented.* They are constantly in motion. They manage by wandering around and by keeping their fingers on the pulse of their departments or companies.

Having the Resolve to Move Quickly

When you learn a new idea, resolve to take action on it immediately. There is a direct relationship between how quickly you take action on a new idea and how likely it is that you will ever take action on any new idea at all. If it works, you have learned a new skill. If it doesn't work immediately, you get feedback that enables you to self-correct and move ahead.

Here now are seventeen management principles you must learn to apply to your company and your team.

Principle 1: Clarity Is Essential

Perhaps the best definition of management is "getting results through others." Management is not doing it yourself with the assistance of the people around you. Management is getting the job done through others.

As we discussed in Chapter 8, the greatest demotivator in the world of work is not knowing what's expected. Conversely, the greatest motivator of human performance is when people know exactly what is expected of them. Your chief responsibility as a manager is to be absolutely clear about what it is you are trying to do and how you are trying to do it, and then making the job responsibility of each person who reports to you absolutely clear as well.

There is a rule in time management that says that every minute spent in planning saves ten minutes in execution.

Every minute that you spend thinking through and developing absolute clarity about your goals and objectives, and then conveying them to others through discussion and feedback, will save you ten minutes in getting the result that you desire.

Fully 80 percent of your success in business and in life is going to be determined by your level of clarity in every area. Effective managers know exactly what they are trying to accomplish, and everyone who reports to them is crystal clear about what they are expected to do to achieve the overall goal. Ineffective managers are unclear about their responsibilities and, as a result, the people below them are unclear as well. This leads to enormous amounts of wasted time and effort.

Clarity is the starting point of becoming an outstanding manager.

Principle 2: Competence Is Critical

Your employees will not be motivated to do as you ask or follow your lead if they have any questions about your competence as a manager and a leader of the unit. Others must see that you commit to excellence in the most important things that you do. Specifically, you commit yourself and your organization to be the best in the critical areas that are most important to your customers.

This is the hallmark of outstanding managers. They are absolutely dedicated to doing the job in a superb fashion. We are living in the most competitive business environment in all of human history today and only those individuals and organizations that produce products and services in an excellent way will survive. This must be your central focus.

Begin by setting high standards for your own performance. You must lead by example. Only ask others to do things that you have demonstrated that you are willing to do yourself. Then set equally high standards for the people around you. If necessary, ruthlessly discipline and weed out incompetent people.

Learning to Accept Feedback and Self-Correct

The best managers are always asking their customers for feedback and ideas. Both customer compliments and customer complaints are invaluable in telling you what to do more of and what to do less of. One mark of peak performers is that they accept feedback and self-correct. Continually scan your environment like radar scans the horizon, looking for ways that you can improve what you are doing.

Here is a key question for you to ask and answer for the rest of your career: What one thing, if we did it in an excellent fashion, would have the greatest positive impact on our business?

Whatever your answer to that question, write it down, make a plan, set standards of performance, get organized, and begin working, every single day, to perform that task in an outstanding fashion. This commitment alone can change your entire life and the entire future of your business.

Principle 3: Identify Your Constraints

This is one of the most important concepts in modern management. The principle of constraints says that, between you and any goal you want to achieve, there is a specific constraint that sets the *speed* at which you achieve that goal. This constraint is often called a bottleneck or choke point. Sometimes you can think of this constraint as the *limiting factor* between where you are and where you want to go.

For example, if you want to increase your sales volume, the critical constraint could be the number of customers that you attract to your business. Or perhaps the critical constraint is the quality of the customers that you attract. Or perhaps the constraint is the loyalty of the customers that you attract. Or perhaps it is the number of possible resales and referrals you can get from the customers you attract.

The best leaders accurately identify the constraint that determines how fast they achieve their goal; they are then prepared to try a different approach or a different strategy to overcome the constraint.

Internal versus External Constraints

Constraints follow the 80/20 rule. Eighty percent of the constraints on you achieving your goals, either personally or in business, come from *inside* of you or your organization. Only 20 percent are from the *outside.*

This realization marks a major difference between high-performance and low-performance managers. High-performance managers always begin by looking on the inside, by looking at their staff, their organizational structure, their products, their services, their business processes, their advertising, their sales, marketing, and so on, for the factors that are holding them back. Mediocre managers always blame their internal problems on external constraints. But constraints from the outside are seldom the case.

Here's the question: What one constraint, if you could alleviate it completely, could help you move toward your goal faster than anything else? What one problem, if you could solve it, would help you the most in achieving your most important business goals? What one goal, if you could achieve it, would help you the most in your business?

Whatever your answer is to that question, begin focusing all of your energies on relieving that constraint today. It could change the entire future of your business.

Principle 4: Unlock Your Creativity

Leaders who are overwhelmed by problems and seem unable to reach their goals will demotivate the rest of the team. What's the use of trying, people will say, when even the boss is stuck? The most inspiring leaders aren't fazed by problems. They resolve them in a timely, focused manner and keep moving toward their goals.

Here is some good news. According to all the science and research, you are a *potential* genius. You have within you incredible reserves of brain power that you habitually fail to use. You probably have sufficient knowledge and intelligence, right now, to overcome any obstacle, solve any problem, and achieve any goal that you can set for yourself.

To unlock your inner genius, you need three things: (1) intensely desired goals, (2) pressing problems, and (3) focused questions. One good idea is all you need to change the future of your business and your life, and you stimulate these ideas by focusing and concentrating your mind on your goals, your problems, or on key questions.

The Twenty Ideas Method

Here is a simple exercise that can change your life. Take a sheet of paper and write your biggest current goal or problem at the top of the page in the form of a question. For example, you could write, "How can we double our sales over the next twenty-four months?"

You then force yourself to write twenty answers to that question. This is not easy the first time you do it. Nonetheless, by disciplining yourself to write at least twenty answers to the question, you will be absolutely surprised at the quality of the answers that begin appearing on the page before you.

Once you have twenty answers, go over the list and select

one answer that you then implement immediately. The faster you implement this idea, the more other ideas will come to you.

Then ask yourself this question on a regular basis: What one problem, if I were to solve it, would have the greatest positive impact on my business? Whatever your answer is to that single problem, write it down, develop twenty answers, and then take action. You will be amazed at the results.

Principle 5: Concentrate Single-Mindedly

Some skills are helpful to succeeding as a manager and a leader, and some skills are *essential.* Your ability to concentrate single-mindedly on one thing at a time is perhaps more important than any other skill or discipline that you can develop in your entire career.

How can you motivate other people if they don't know if your focus today will be your focus tomorrow? Why should people try to do their best on a vital activity that you may decide later is not so important?

All successful men and women have developed the ability to concentrate on their most important task and to stay with it until it is done. Unsuccessful, mediocre men and women diffuse their efforts and try to do too many things at once, and they end up doing nothing particularly well.

Try asking and answering four questions, every hour of every day, to keep yourself on track:

1. *What are my highest value activities?* You must be absolutely clear about the things you do that contribute the greatest value to your business and to your life, and then work on those activities, all day long.

2. *Why am I on the payroll?* What exactly have you been hired to accomplish? Why do they pay you money at work?

What specific results do you have to achieve, day after day, to justify your paycheck? Whatever your answers to this question, work on them every single day.

3. *What can I, and only I do, that if I do it well, will make a real difference?* This is one of the greatest time management questions of all, and there is only one answer at any given time. There has to be something that only you can do. If you don't do it, it won't get done. But if you do it, and do it well, it can make an enormous difference. What is it?

Whatever your answer to that question, it should be your top priority every minute, every hour of every day.

4. *What is the most valuable use of my time, right now?* Every minute, every hour, there is only one answer to this question in time management and concentration. Your job is to organize your time and your life so that you are focusing single-mindedly on that one task that can make more of a difference in your work and your career than any other task. This is the key to concentration.

Principle 6: Have the Courage of Your Convictions

Courage is the second most common characteristic or quality of the true leader. To succeed greatly, you must develop the courage to take risks, to move out of your comfort zone, and to try things with no guarantee of success. In study after study, top managers have been found to be those who were willing to step out in faith and to reach for something higher and better, even though there was always the possibility of frustration, failure, and disappointment.

As a young man, I learned something that changed my life. It is this: Everyone is afraid. Everyone is afraid of lots of things. We are afraid of failure. We are afraid of criticism. We are afraid of disapproval. We are afraid of financial or personal loss. We are afraid of embarrassment or ridicule. We are afraid of lots of things. But if we allow our fears to dominate our thinking, we will never do anything worthwhile.

Glenn Ford, the actor, once said, "If you do not do the thing you fear, then the fear controls your life." A brave person is not a person without fear. It is a person who acts in spite of the fear. Ralph Waldo Emerson wrote these wonderful words: "If you would be a great success, make a habit throughout your life of doing the things you fear. If you do the thing you fear, the death of fear is certain."

What One Great Thing?

Courage in management does not mean jumping out of an airplane without a parachute. It means that you think, plan, gather information, and realize that it is safer to go forward into the unknown than to play it safe with the tried-and-true methods, products, and services of yesterday. And it seems that, if you act boldly, unseen forces will come to your aid.

So consider this question: What one great thing would you dare to dream, if you knew you could not fail? If you had no fears of failure whatsoever, of any kind, what goal would you set for yourself and what actions would you take? Whatever your answer to this question, write it down, make a plan, and begin working on it today.

Principle 7: Develop Your Character

Your character, your *reputation*, is the most important quality you develop throughout your career. Shakespeare wrote, "He who steals my purse steals trash; but he who steals my good name, steals all."

Shakespeare also wrote, "To thine own self be true, and

then it must follow, as the night the day, thou canst not then be false to any man."

What we are talking about here is *integrity*. Be impeccably honest with yourself and others. Live in truth with yourself and always tell the truth to others. Never compromise your integrity for any short-term gain, of any kind. Integrity is the most required and respect quality of leadership. It is the key to rapid advancement. It is essential to earning the respect, esteem, and loyalty of the people around you.

Leaders are fastidious about developing and maintaining their reputations for high levels of honesty and integrity. So, always do the right thing. Listen to your intuition, your inner voice, and always do what you know to be right and good and fair in every situation. Your commitment to integrity also has a direct effect on your level of self-confidence, self-esteem, and self-respect.

Principle 8: Plan Every Detail in Advance

Planning is one of the key result areas of management. Your ability to plan, to think through what needs to be done, in advance, on paper, is a critical skill that largely determines your entire future. Your job is to determine *what* is to be done. The jobs of your staff members are to determine *how* it is to be done, and where and when and with what resources. But your job is to determine the "what" of the job. Only you can set the plan.

The key to planning is for you to be very clear about the results expected. You then make a list of everything that you have to do to achieve those results. You organize your list in terms of priority. You calculate the resources, especially the people and money that will be necessary to achieve those goals. You then lay out this plan with such clarity and simplicity that, like a blueprint for a house, another person can take it and put it together.

Your ability to plan your goals with great clarity will do more to determine your success than any other single factor. Take the time to do it right.

Principle 9: Organize Your Work Before You Begin

The job of organizing in management means bringing together all the necessary resources you need to get the job done. Once you have laid out your plan and know exactly what it is that you want to accomplish and everything you need to accomplish it, you then begin assembling the people, money, and other resources you've identified so you can achieve that goal or result.

In organizing, you determine exactly how much money you need. You determine the people you will need and the skills and abilities of those people. You determine your facility and real estate requirements. You determine what furniture, equipment, information technology, and other essential supplies or resources you need.

In organizing, you then plan the work like a project, with specific functions and responsibilities, delegated to specific people to be accomplished at specific times and to specific standards of performance.

Planning and organizing are the critical tools of the high-performance manager. And the more you practice them, the better you get at them and the more results you accomplish.

Principle 10: Staff Properly at Every Level

This is where the rubber meets the road. Ninety-five percent of your success as a manager will be determined by the people you select or keep to help you to do the job.

As discussed in Chapter 7, most people promoted into management have never been trained in the processes of effective interviewing and selection of staff. As a result, much hiring is done haphazardly, on an intuitive basis. But today, with talent at a premium and competition at an all-time high level of intensity, you have to be able to make good staffing decisions from the very beginning.

When you are getting ready to hire a person, but before you begin the job search, sit down with a piece of paper and write out a list of all of the qualities, characteristics, and abilities that the ideal person would have. Review your list with other people who might be working with this person and make additions and deletions until it is complete. Then, you begin your process of selection by comparing candidates against the list that you have developed. This exercise alone will help you weed out people and lead you to the highest-quality candidates from which to select.

By the way, one of the major reasons that managers fail is because they are unable to replace incompetent staff members for fear of hurting their feelings. If you have a person on your staff who either cannot or will not do the job, you must act quickly to replace that person with someone who will. This is a chief responsibility of management.

Principle 11: Delegate Effectively

This is another area where very few managers receive any training. But the art of delegation fills many books and has been written about extensively in hundreds of articles. In fact, your ability to delegate effectively is the key to success. Without the ability to delegate well, you have no future as a manager. You must eventually go back to the ranks. A person who cannot delegate must be replaced by someone who can.

Fortunately, you can learn to be excellent at delegation. The keys to it are quite simple: First, think through the task that needs to be done, in advance of delegating. Second, select the person to do the task carefully, on the basis of that person's previous experience and current abilities. Third, discuss the task thoroughly with the other person and get the other person to provide you with feedback about what he perceives the task to be. Fourth, offer to help the individual in every way possible by providing support in the form of people, money, and resources to do the job. And fifth, remember that delegation is not *abdication*. You are still responsible. Arrange to check with the staff member on a regular basis to make sure that everything is proceeding according to plan.

Poor delegation has led to the defeat of great armies and to the collapse of great enterprises. Delegate carefully. Delegate patiently. Delegate thoroughly. Delegate with care and with sensitivity. And study delegation as part of your professional development for the rest of your career.

Principle 12: Inspect What You Expect

Once you have planned and organized, staffed and delegated, you must supervise your people to make sure they get the job done on time and on budget.

Perhaps the best supervision technique today is called "management by wandering around." This is where you spend 75 percent of your time moving among your people, talking to them, asking them questions, getting feedback, and making suggestions. All the best managers are visible most of the time to their staff, and they are always available if their staff members have a problem or question. By continually interacting with your staff, you get regular and timely feedback. You keep your finger on the pulse of operations. You are never surprised or blindsided.

The best managers *manage by objectives.* Each and every staff member knows exactly what it is that he is supposed to be doing, and to what standard and by what deadline. The manager then asks, on a regular basis, "How is it going?"

The manager positions herself as a helper, as a teacher, as a resource whose job it is to help the employee get the job done. The manager is continually looking out for her staff to make sure that they have what they need to perform at their best.

Perhaps the most important thing you do as a manager is to continually encourage and motivate your staff. Tell them that they are doing a good job. Thank them for everything and anything that they do that is at all out of the ordinary. Smile at them when you see them and listen to them carefully when they talk. Praise them in front of others and at staff meetings. Create an environment where people feel terrific about themselves.

Principle 13: Keep the Boss Informed

People who get paid more and promoted faster are almost invariably those who report with greater clarity and regularity on their activities to the people around them. Yet it is not enough for you to do a good job and get results in a timely fashion. You must pass this information on quickly to the people whose opinions are important to you, especially the people above you.

Senior managers like to practice what is called a "no surprises" policy. The people above you do not like surprises of any kind. If something happens out of the ordinary, tell them quickly and clearly what has happened and what you are going to do to resolve it.

Your boss is either a *visual* or an *auditory* person in terms of preferred reporting style. A visual person wants everything written down. Auditory people want you to tell them aloud. Find out which way your boss prefers to get information. Then, forever after, make sure that you report to your boss in the manner that your boss is most comfortable receiving information. This can make an enormous difference in your career.

Principle 14: Focus on High Productivity

This is a key result area of management. You are responsible for getting the job done, whatever it is. In its strictest terms, *productivity* means continually looking for ways to increase the level of outputs versus inputs, to increase the quantity and quality of products and services being produced while holding the costs of production constant or even lowering those costs.

To maintain ever-higher levels of productivity, you must be continually looking for ways to get the job done faster, better, cheaper, easier, and more efficiently than ever before. You must instill a culture of continuous improvement in the staff around you. Every day in every way, you and everyone around you must be looking for ways to do the job quicker and better.

The three R's for attaining higher productivity are reorganization, reengineering, and restructuring:

- *Reorganization* requires that you continually move people around so that they are getting more and more higher-value tasks done.
- *Reengineering* requires that you continually analyze the process that you use to get results and then simplify this process so that it is smoother and more efficient. Look for

ways to reduce the number of steps or complexity of any task, thereby reducing the time and cost necessary to do it. This effort can lead to greater efficiency and considerable savings.

■ *Restructuring* requires you to continually move your most important people and resources to those areas where they can produce the highest-value products and services for your customers. You continually focus on the 20 percent of tasks, products, services, and activities that account for 80 percent of the results and rewards in your business.

The more productively you organize the work, the more motivated people are to do the work. And the more motivated they are, the more they produce, and the better you look as a manager.

Principle 15: Commit to Quality in Everything

Personal competence is critical (principle number two), but quality is something else. Quality has to do with developing an area of excellence, a competitive advantage for your product or service that makes what you sell stand out from all other rival offerings in the marketplace.

Employees who are happy and motivated are usually proud of the products and services they offer to their customers. On the other, employees working in companies that have a cavalier attitude about the quality of their products or services are hardly motivated to do their best.

The best market research you can do is to ask your customers how *they* define quality in terms of your products and services. Many individuals and organizations concentrate on improving quality in areas that the customer doesn't care about at all. Ask your customers why they buy from you rather than from someone else. Then, whatever reason they give for their buying decision, focus all of your energies on getting even better in that key decision area.

Set not only standards of performance in your business, but standards of *excellent* performance. The highest profit companies, based on more than twenty years of research, have a reputation for quality products and services that are better than their competitors.

Two factors influence how customers define the quality of products and services. The first is the product or service itself. The second, and often more important factor, is the way that the product or service is sold and delivered to the customer by the people in the company. The very best companies sell not only good products and services, but they sell them in a friendly, cheerful, and customer-oriented way. So should you.

Look around you and ask yourself this question: What one area, if we were the absolute quality leader in that area, would have the greatest impact on the future of this business?

Whatever it is, focus your energies on becoming absolutely outstanding in that one product or service area. It could change the entire future of your business.

Principle 16: Concentrate on Continuous Improvement

People are motivated and enthusiastic if they are working toward an ideal. Not just an ideal of the self, but also an ideal of the organization for which they work.

Organizational development embraces all of the factors that go into building a company. It includes the selection of products and services; the decisions about particular markets; the scope of activities of the company; the recruiting, training, and management policies of the people in the company; the decisions with regard to leadership and strategy, finances, labor policies, internal culture, and many other things.

An exercise that successful leaders do regularly in strategic planning is to ask the top team of executives to describe the company as it would be if it were *perfect* five years from today. You can do this exercise for your business as well.

Go around the room and have each manager "idealize" the company by writing down a description of how the company would look and how it would be talked about in five years if the company were the finest company in its industry. Once you have a list of clear definitions of the ideal future vision of the company, then organize these definitions by priority and begin developing plans. Begin strategizing on how you could change and develop certain parts of the organization to be sure that, in five years, these goals are realized.

Principle 17: Innovate Continually

Is your company on the move or stagnant? Do you have the cutting-edge products in the industry or are you the laggard? People are inspired by working for a company that innovates continually and that is always searching for the next best way to do something.

Invest time and money in research and development aimed at creating new products and services. Most of the top companies aim to have 20 percent of their revenues coming each year from products that have been developed in the last twenty-four months. Continually think and plan as though your best-selling product or service was on the verge of becoming obsolete and knocked out of the market. What is your next big product or service going to be?

Hold regular brainstorming meetings with your staff. Agree to a simple question that you write on the whiteboard or on a flip chart. Then, take fifteen to thirty minutes and concentrate on generating the greatest number of creative ideas to solve that problem or achieve that goal. When you hold regular brainstorming sessions with your staff, you will be absolutely amazed at the incredible ideas and insights that average people have that can move your business forward at a rapid rate.

Keep asking yourself, "If we were not now doing it this way, would we start it up again this same way today?" Or, "Could there be a better way to do it than the way we are doing it currently?"

Study your most successful competitors and find ways to copy their most successful practices. Benchmark your performance against the performance of the most successful people in your industry. Set high standards for yourself and continually look for ways to meet and exceed those standards. Ideas and innovation are the keys to twenty-first-century business success, and the critical determinants of your success as a manager.

Wrapping Up

Let me summarize this chapter with a couple of thoughts. First, this is the very best time in all of human history to be alive. In times of market turbulence and market retrenchment, there are more opportunities and possibilities for you to demonstrate your skills and abilities and to move up through the ranks of management to leadership.

In this chapter, I have touched upon seventeen of the most important practices of highly effective managers. You should review these points and give yourself a grade from 1 to 10 on how well you think you are doing in each of these areas. Your weakest important skill is usually what is holding you back from using all of your other skills at their highest level.

Your job is to identify the areas where you are weak, where you could improve, and then develop a plan to get better in one key area. When you hear a lot of good ideas, like you have here, your natural tendency will be to want to begin improving in a whole lot of areas at once. But that would be counterproductive. It is much better for you to pick a single skill area where you feel that you can make a significant difference and then to concentrate on that one skill until you have mastered it.

Just Do It!

Remember, all successful managers are oriented to results, solutions, and actions. But the most important quality of effective managers is that they are action-oriented. When they think of an idea or see an opportunity, they take action on it immediately. When they hear a good idea, they move quickly. They have a sense of urgency. They have a bias for action. They practice fast tempo in everything they do. And so should you.

The primary reason that people do not grow in management is that they don't try anything new. They get stuck in a comfort zone. They keep doing things the same old way and wonder why they are getting the same old results. You should review this chapter on a regular basis and take from it a single idea each time you feel you need help the most, and then implement that idea immediately. Do it now! Move fast when an idea occurs to you.

Here's the good news. The faster you move, the more energy you have. The faster you move, the more feedback you get. The faster you move, the better results you get and the better you feel about yourself. The faster you move, the greater an impact you have on other people. The faster you move, the more confidence and courage you have and the faster you become one of the outstanding managers of your generation.

Good luck!

Index

Build a Great Business!

Brian Tracy's Total Business Mastery Seminar
(2 ½ Day Live Seminar / Workshop)

In this two and a half day Total Business Mastery Seminar, Brian Tracy and his team of experts not only expand on the revolutionary ideas in this book, but cover three additional powerful principles of business.

In this live training you cover each area of *Now, Build a Great Business!* in further detail while you work on your own personal Action Guide.

You'll work on your business and mastermind with peers and experts about your strengths, weaknesses, challenges, and greatest opportunities. You'll leave this seminar with a written plan to increase your sales, reduce your costs, and boost your profits.

Plus, you learn how to become a more effective executive and generate the critical numbers essential for business success.

You learn and internalize the 10 GREAT areas of business success, becoming one of the best businesspeople of your generation.

This entire program can be presented, with all materials, to individuals, corporations and organizations of almost any size.

For more information go to:
www.briantracy.com/tbm
or call 858 436-7300

Learn the practical, proven skills and techniques that you need to survive, thrive and grow in any business and in any market

FREE Resources – From Brian Tracy

*Brian Tracy has created these resources to help you get
a step ahead in your business and your life.*

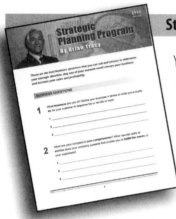

Strategic Planning Business Blueprint PDF

You don't have to be a certified business guru to know
what's working within your business and what's not.
Having a clear and detailed strategic plan is the basis
of your business success. This detailed and practical
strategic planning guide will help you identify your
goals and create a business blueprint for achieving
them – faster than ever before!

12-Step Goal-Setting Process Plus Exercise

In planning for success you always start with yourself and
your personal goals. Your work and your business life are
what you do so you can enjoy the most important parts
of your life – your family and your relationships.

This 12-Step Goal-Setting Process and Goal-Setting
Exercise will help you determine what is really
important to you so that you can make better
decisions in your business and personal life.

Visit www.briantracy.com/FEresources

About the Author

Brian Tracy is a professional speaker, trainer, seminar leader, and consultant and is the chairman of Brian Tracy International, a training and consulting company based in Solana Beach, California. He is also a self-made millionaire.

Brian learned his lessons the hard way. He left high school without graduating and worked as a laborer for several years. In his mid-twenties he became a salesman and began his climb up the business ladder. Year by year, studying and applying every idea, method, and technique he could find, he worked his way up to become chief operating officer of a $276-million development company.

In 1981 he began teaching his success principles in talks and seminars around the country. Today, his books, audio programs, and video seminars have been translated into 38 languages and are used in 55 countries.

He is the bestselling author of more than fifty books, including *Maximum Achievement, Advanced Selling Strategies, Focal Point*, and *The 100 Absolutely Unbreakable Laws of Business Success.* He has written and produced more than 500 audio and video learning programs that are used worldwide.

Brian is happily married and has four children.

Brian Tracy

Speaker • Trainer • Seminar Leader

Brian is one of the top professional speakers in the world, addressing more than 250,000 people in over a hundred appearances each year throughout the United States, Europe, Asia, and Australia. His keynote speeches, talks, and seminars are described as "inspiring, entertaining, informative, and motivational," and his audiences include businesses and associations of every size and type, including many Fortune 500 companies. Since he began speaking professionally, Brian has shared his ideas with more than five million people in 58 countries, and has served as a consultant and trainer for more than 1,000 corporations. He has lived and practiced every principle in this book.

21st Century Thinking – How to outthink, outplan, and outstrategize your competition and get superior results in a turbulent, fast-changing business environment.

Leadership in the New Millennium – How to apply the most powerful leadership principles ever discovered to manage, motivate, and get better results, faster than ever before.

Advanced Selling Strategies – How to outthink, outperform, and outsell your competition using the most advanced strategies and tactics know to modern selling.

The Psychology of Success – How the top people think and act in every area of personal and business life. You'll learn countless practical, proven methods and strategies for peak performance.

For full information on booking Brian to speak at your next meeting or conference, visit Brian Tracy International at www.briantracy.com, or call 858 436-7300 for a free promotional package. Brian will carefully customize his talk for you and for your needs.